The Reappearance of the Christ
and
the Masters of Wisdom

BENJAMIN CREME

The Reappearance of the Christ
and
the Masters of Wisdom

BENJAMIN CREME

THE TARA PRESS - London
TARA CENTER - Los Angeles

TARA CENTER

P.O. Box 6001, North Hollywood, CA 91603 U.S.A.

THE TARA PRESS

59 Dartmouth Park Road, London NW5 1SL, England

ISBN 0-936604-00-X

(formerly ISBN 0 9566797 0 4 when published in Gt. Britain)

Library of Congress Catalog Number 80-50639

The painting reproduced on the cover was painted by Benjamin Creme in 1973/4. Entitled "Chalice", it represents the Cosmic Spiritual Heart Centre whose nature is Fire and from which flows that energy we call Love.

To my Revered Master
without Whose Overshadowing
Presence this book could not
have been written.

ACKNOWLEDGEMENTS

The author's name is on the cover and the contents were written or spoken by him, but this book is, in the fullest sense, the result of group effort. The long and arduous task of listening to scores of tapes and transcribing the many hundreds of questions and answers from which the final selection was made, the typing and photocopying, was cheerfully and efficiently undertaken by the group with which he works. The author wishes to convey his grateful thanks to the following: Dick Benson; Roy Bowden; Tony Cartwright; Phyllis Creme, his wife; Julian Creme, his son; Michael D'Addio, whose idea it was that a book existed in these tapes; Felicity Eliot; Joan Foubister; Cy Laurie; Pat Maitland, typist; Judith and Robert Noble-Warren; Maarten van Rossum, for his invaluable help in editing the material; Valerie and Jennie Stock and Caroline Tosh.

Note to Reader: The reader should note that all numerical dates are expressed in the following order: day, month, year.

CONTENTS

PREFACE

MANY PEOPLE HAVE asked me to relate something of the steps which have led me into the work I am now doing. It will not be a complete account: there are unwritten laws of reticence on some aspects of the Master-Disciple relationship, and I am pledged to silence on certain work for and with the Space Brothers; but for whatever interest it may have, and in the hope that it may make more real and believable the fact of the Masters and the fact of the Christ's return at Their head, I set down the following:

As a child of four or five, one of my favourite pastimes was to sit at the window and watch the wind; not the effect of the wind on the trees or leaves, but the wind itself. I would watch the movements of the air and try to guess whether it was a north, south, east or west wind blowing. When I went to school, I learned that the air was invisible, the wind likewise, and forgot, I do not remember whether gradually or suddenly, my ability to see what of course was some level of the etheric planes of matter.

Above the dense physical—solid, liquid, and gaseous—are four planes of still finer matter which constitute the etheric envelope of this planet, and of which the dense physical planes are a precipitation. It was not until some twenty years later, through the building and use of Wilhelm Reich's orgone accumulator, that I again became aware of this ocean of energy of which we ourselves are a part, and proved to myself conclusively the existence of the etheric planes.

At the age of fourteen, I read what was for me an extraordinary book: *With Mystics and Magicians in Tibet,* by Alexandra David Neel. This Polish woman of indefatigable courage, determination and resource managed, disguised as a Lama, to penetrate the forbidding barriers around that mysterious country, gained permission to stay, and placed herself under

11

the tutorship of a true Lama. She describes various esoteric practices, some of which she learned, including the creation by thought of a "familiar"; in her case of a jovial fat monk who soon got out of her control and had to be de-materialised. These practices obviously involved considerable concentration and mind control, but I found a little success with some of them, including Tumo, a system for creating internal heat in cold weather.

In the late 1940s, through a study of Wilhelm Reich's work, and the use of the orgone accumulator, I became consciously aware of, and extremely sensitive to, energy currents; so much so that eventually I could tell when an atomic bomb had been exploded in the Pacific or wherever. Across these thousands of miles, I registered the shift in the etheric currents caused by the explosions. Inevitably, a day or two later, would come the report that America, Russia, or Britain had tested a "device" of such and such a size.

In the early 1950s, I happened on a book by Rolf Alexander: *The Power of the Mind*. The magazine article which drew my attention to it had, of course, concentrated on the most sensational aspect of the book—"cloud-busting", the breaking up of clouds by the power of thought alone. Rolf Alexander, a Canadian, was called to Tibet and trained by a Tibetan Master of Yoga, and his book outlines a practice to bring the instinctive, subconscious mind under the control of the directive conscious mind. The latter is only too often fragmented and partly submerged in the subconscious computer activity of the former, and a great deal of its available energy is lost. The method used is self-hypnosis. The freeing of the conscious, directing principle from its involvement in the activity of the subconscious mind (which should proceed automatically) releases large stores of mental energy and leads directly to the focus and concentration which precede meditation. And so I began to meditate.

I also began to read. I read, among many others, the Theosophical works of H. P. Blavatsky and Leadbeater; Gurdjieff, Ouspensky and Nicoll; Paul Brunton; Patanjali; the Alice Bailey and Agni Yoga Teachings; Swamis Vivekananda,

Sivananda, Yogananda; Sri Ramana Maharshi, whose Path of Self-knowledge I sought to follow. Through His meditation on "Who am I?" (and, I know now, through the Grace of my Master), I found myself precipitated into a sense of identity with the whole phenomenal world: the earth, the sky, the houses and people; the trees and birds and clouds, I saw to be myself. I disappeared as a separate being, yet retained full consciousness, a consciousness expanded to include everything. I saw that this was the true Reality, that one's normal waking consciousness simply covers this, keeps it hidden, through wrong identification with oneself as this body. I also saw this phenomenal world as a kind of ritual, a ritualised shadow-play, acting out a dream or desire of That which alone existed, alone was Real, which was also myself.

Around 1953, I read Desmond Leslie's and George Adamski's *Flying Saucers have Landed* and Adamski's *Inside the Space Ships*, which made a deep impression, and had for me, the ring of truth. Until then, I had looked on reports of flying saucers as probably referring to secret new types of aeroplanes being built by America and Russia. My reactions to these books I think can be summarised as: The Space People are obviously here. It would be marvellous to meet them, but if they want me I am sure they will know where to find me. Until that time it does not concern me.

In mid-1957, I began to work with a society involved with the U.F.O. phenomenon, which claimed contact with the Space Brothers. With this group I did my first public speaking, but more importantly, discovered my ability to transmit the cosmic spiritual energies from the Space People, which was a major work of the group. I also found I could heal.

Towards the end of 1958 I withdrew from this society and entered into the closest contact with, and work for, the Space Brothers. The nature of this work I am afraid I may not reveal, but many misconceptions about them and their activities which I had held were rectified at this time. I worked very briefly with George Adamski during a visit he paid to this country, and can vouch for the authenticity of his contacts from my own experience.

13

How did I come into this work? In late 1958, I was told by a fellow disciple who had the "connection", that I was receiving "messages". This surprised me and I had no sense that it was true. I was told that the messages "bounced off" me, but if I did such and such, in time I would receive correctly.

I must have done the right thing, because one night, early in January 1959, so clearly there was no mistaking, I heard inwardly the instruction: Go to so and so (a place in London) on such and such a date and time, some three weeks ahead. On the night, there were people waiting there to meet me.

That was the start of a flow of messages which came in gathering momentum. Some, apparently, I missed (I was told later when I missed one) and I became so afraid of missing them that I gave them to myself. I sent myself on several rendezvous, where nothing happened and no one came, but gradually I settled down; I did not miss them and I stopped making them up.

I was told to get a tape-recorder and received many long dictations of various kinds. Some contained advice, guidance, or spiritual instruction. I was not told the identity of the Master (or Masters) Who spoke thus, telepathically, to me, and I think I was too shy to ask, although I was told I could ask questions. It was not until years later that I learned His name and also that I would have been told had I asked long ago.

One night, early in 1959, during such a transmission, I was told to turn off the tape-recorder. There followed a discourse on His Reappearance by Maitreya, the Christ, Head of our planetary Hierarchy. He said also that I would have a part in the Plan. At that time I believed that the World Teacher would come from one of the higher planets, probably from Venus, and this information from Maitreya caused a complete upset to my thinking. In a transmission soon after this event, my Master, referring to this new-found knowledge, added: **"The time is coming when you will be expected to act upon it."** And in another: **"Affirm His coming!"**

I cannot claim that I took these exhortations to heart and that that is why I am engaged in this work of preparation for the Christ. On instruction, I put these tapes away for seventeen years and I am afraid I needed a rather strong push from the Master to launch me into this work.

Towards the end of 1972, when I was rather in the doldrums and least expecting it, that Wise and Wily, One Whom I have the privilege to call Master, pounced. He took me in hand, and subjected me to the most intensive period of de-glamorisation, disillusioning, training and preparation. For months we worked together, twenty hours a day, deepening and strengthening the telepathic link until it was two-way with equal ease, requiring the minimum of His attention and energy. He forged in this period an instrument through whom He could work, and which would be responsive to His slightest impression (of course, with my complete co-operation and without the slightest infringement of my free will). Everything I see and hear, He sees and hears. When He wishes, a look from me can be a look from Him; my touch, His. So, with the minimum expenditure of energy He has a window on the world, an outpost of His consciousness; He can heal and teach. He Himself remains, in a fully physical body, thousands of miles away. I am not suggesting that I am His only "window on the world". I do not know how rare this is, but I am sure that it is not unique. It constitutes a definite stage in the Master-Disciple relationship. He has asked me not to reveal His identity for the time being—not even to the members of the group with which I work, and through which He works. I know of two reasons (there may be others) for His request, and respect them, but I may say that He is one of the Senior Members of the Hierarchy, a Master of the Wisdom, Whose name is well known to esotericists in the West. His inspiration has heightened tremendously the conceptual power and intensity of my paintings.

Two small episodes, among many—which illustrate the loving concern of the Great Ones, and Their lively sense of humour, as well as the ability to use Their powers at long distance:

The first occurred early in 1973, during the period of most intense preparation and training. For some time I had been smoking small cigarlettes, and the Master frequently urged me to stop smoking these "filthy weeds" as He called them. His technique of discouraging me was to assign some meditation or exercise every time I made to light one.

One day, preparing to keep an appointment somewhere, I laid this small box of cigars on the corner of my bed while I changed clothes. When I was ready to leave, it had, literally, disappeared. I asked the Master, of course, if He had done something to it. He claimed complete ignorance of, or interest in, the "filthy weeds". I was certain of where I had left them, but nevertheless made a thorough search, without result. "Are you sure you didn't hide them?" I repeated. He swore His innocence: He had better things to do with His time and energy. At last I said: "All right, I'll just get some more on the way out." Immediately, they lay on the bed-corner where I had left them.

The second episode concerns a bird and occurred about two and a half years ago. Each year, we are visited by large numbers of swifts who dive and wheel outside our windows all day long and nest under the eaves.

Early one hot summer morning, one of these marvellous birds flew through an open bedroom window, straight through the closed venetian blind. It dropped with a thud on to a large tin of floor varnish which stood under the window, bending the handle and top of the tin with the impact. It lay there panting, its eyes staring and its enormous wings lying awry, one on, and one over the side of, the tin. The Master asked me to look closely and carefully over the bird and I felt His energy pouring through my eyes. At once, it relaxed and closed its eyes.

The Master assured me that there were no bones broken, but that it was severely bruised and shocked. He told me to open the window at the bottom and to go down and have breakfast. Half an hour later, I returned to find the bird gone, healed and restored to the morning air.

These two little episodes may surprise those students who remember the Master Djwhal Khul's statement that the Masters are not interested in, and do not concern Themselves with, the personality lives of disciples. While I am sure that, in general, this is true, I am equally certain that there are exceptions to this rule. It depends entirely on the type of relationship

16

the Master is seeking to build, the degree of trust He seeks to elicit, and the karmic relationship existing between Himself and the disciple.

In March 1974, He gave me a list of fourteen names of people to invite to a talk at my home on "meditation and allied subjects". They all came.

I talked about the Hierarchy of Masters, about meditation, and its role in bringing about soul contact. Under instruction, I presented them with the following offer: I invited them to take part in a group work in which their occult meditation would proceed under the guidance of a Master of the Wisdom, in exchange for which they would act as transmitters of the Hierarchical energies, thus forming a bridging group between Hierarchy and the disciples in the field.

The Master arranged a short transmission to show them what was involved. Twelve of the fourteen agreed, two feeling that they were not ready for this kind of work.

The group was formed in March 1974 to channel the spiritual potencies. We met twice weekly, at first, for about 1½–2 hours. The question of a name for the group came up, but the Master's instruction was, and still is, that no name should be used; no organisation built; no officers appointed; no fence erected around ourselves and our ideas; the maximum openness maintained.

At the same time, the Master gave me the blueprint for building the transmitter-transformer instrument which we use in this work, and which I also use in healing. It is a tetrahedron in form and is based on the principle that certain shapes have inherent energetic properties.

A great study is going on today into the nature and energetic properties of the pyramid. The Great Pyramid at Giza is really an Atlantean instrument, based on the power of shape. The aim of Atlantean man was to perfect the astral-emotional vehicle, or body. Just by being the shape it is, the pyramid, when aligned with the north and south poles, draws energy from the etheric and astral planes. This was transmitted for the benefit of the population of the great city which lies buried beneath the sands around the Pyramid and the Sphinx.

17

The aim of our present, fifth, root race, the Aryan, is to perfect the mental vehicle. When aligned north and south, the Tetrahedron automatically draws to itself and transmits energy from the mental planes. This principle is behind our use of the instrument. The instrumentation—quartz crystal, magnets, gold and silver discs and wires, focuses and potentises all the energies channelled through us by Hierarchy; the shape itself transforming them downwards on to the lower mental planes where they can be more readily absorbed by many people. Without this transforming work, which the instrument carries further, the Hierarchical energies, streaming as they do in the main from the Buddhic level (the level of the Spiritual Intuition), would "bounce off" the masses of people, and their effect would be limited. This is behind the need of Hierarchy for transmission groups, using some form of meditation or prayer.

Under the Master's instruction, I built also a Spiritual Energy Battery which can be attached to the transmitter. So far we have used it only once, to demonstrate, I suppose, the principle.

The group's personnel has changed many times, only four of the original group remaining. Its numbers have grown and fallen, but always seem to stabilise at around twelve fully active members, with many less active or regular participants, and a great many offshoots, both here and abroad. Nowadays, we meet regularly three times weekly to transmit the energies from Hierarchy for anything from four to seven or eight hours on end. Only the most dedicated and committed people, of course, can maintain that intensity of rhythm, so numbers are, necessarily, kept low. In addition, we hold a regular weekly public meeting at the Friends Meeting House, Euston Road, London, in which the audience is invited to share in the transmission of the energies which are sent then.

In June 1974 began a series of overshadowing and transmitted messages by Maitreya, inspiring us, and keeping us informed of the progress of His externalisation. We were privileged also to become aware of the gradual creation and perfectionment of His body of manifestation—the Mayavirupa. In the period from March 1976 to September 1977, these communications from Maitreya became very frequent indeed.

During the first year of the group's life, we held an open meeting at each full moon where interested friends of the members could join in the transmission. At these full-moon meetings, I would give a short talk, usually about the reappearance of the Christ and the Hierarchy of Masters, or, on occasion, on the significance, from an esoteric astrological point of view, of the particular full-moon energies. Towards the end of 1974, the Master said, several times: "You know, you must take all this to the public. It is of little use giving this information to the twenty or so people, only, who are here." The pantomime began: I would remonstrate, plead not to have to "go public". He would assure me that He was only joking: "I have other plans for you", He would say, and I would relax again. But in January, 1975, He finally said: "I mean it. Give this information (He had dictated a mass of information on how the Plan would work out) to the groups, of all backgrounds and teachings. Tell them what you know. The hope is that from the more focused minds of the groups will go out a telepathic interplay with the general public, so that when you go to them, they will be somewhat prepared."

I didn't like it. I didn't like it at all. I liked what I was doing. I liked working quietly, esoterically, knowing I was doing something useful, but neither too strenuous nor making too great psychological demands on me. I did nothing about the groups until several firm pushes from the Master at last got me moving. In March or April I wrote hopefully to forty or so groups working along spiritual lines, offering my services as a speaker on: "The Reappearance of the Christ and the Masters of the Wisdom". The response, not surprisingly, for I was quite unknown, was not altogether overwhelming. I had, I think, about six or seven replies. Three of these groups were interested to know more—all newish groups run by young people—Centre House, Gentle Ghost and the Franklin School, and I gave a talk at each, the first at Centre House, on May 30th 1975.

I was very nervous. Although I knew my material, I did not have it in any sort of order. The Master, in His kindness, dictated for me a list of headings which I could glance at, and, in fact, so overshadowed me throughout the talk, that He practically gave it. Just before the end, I was suddenly overshadowed by Maitreya Himself, my heart melted, and I had the greatest difficulty in keeping my voice steady. The following words were put into my mind:

"When the Christ returns, He will not at first reveal His Presence, nor will the Masters Who precede Him; but gradually, steps will be taken which will reveal to men that there lives among them now a man of outstanding, extraordinary, potency, capacity for love and service, and with a breadth of view, far beyond the ordinary. Men and women, all over the world, will find themselves drawn into the awareness of the point in the modern world wherein this man will live; and from that centre of force will flow the True Spirit of the Christ, which will gradually reveal to men that He is with us. Those who can respond to His Presence and His Teaching will find themselves somewhat reflecting this love, this potency, this breadth of vision, and will go into the world and spread abroad the fact that the Christ is in the world, and that men should look to that country from which a certain Teaching is emanating. This will take place in a very, relatively, short period of time, and will lead to conclusive evidence that the Christ is in our midst.

"From that time onwards, the changes which will take place in the world will proceed with a speed unprecedented in the whole history of the planet. The next twenty-five years will show such changes, changes so radical, so fundamental, that the world will be entirely changed for the better."

No one was more surprised than I was to hear this statement. Not until I heard it back on tape was I sure, even, that it made sense.

On July 7th 1977, Maitreya Himself informed us that His body of manifestation—the Mayavirupa—was totally complete, that He had "donned" it, and that His Body of Light (His Ascended Body) was now at rest in His mountain Centre in the Himalayas. On July 8th, we were told, the Descent had begun. On Tuesday, July 19th, my Master told me that Maitreya had now arrived in His "point of focus", a well-known modern country. I had a lecture meeting that night at Friends House, but was told to keep the information to myself, as yet. During our Friday transmission session, the Master told me that Maitreya had been resting, acclimatising Himself, for three days, and that on that day, July 22nd, His Mission had begun. This information I could share with the group.

About midnight, the transmission ended and we congregated as usual for tea before dispersing. My wife turned on the television, where the late-night film featured some family drama with Bette Davis in the leading role. Some of the group watched, but understandably, my thoughts were elsewhere. I made some sarcastic remarks about the film and its actors (usually I admire Bette Davis as an actress very much). When I could bear it no longer, I said I had some rather more important news to tell them—that the Christ was now in the everyday world in full, physical Presence, and beginning His Mission.

Many, many times since, to scores of audiences, I have made this announcement, but never again with the sense of having, even in a small way, shared in a great planetary event. The tears of joy on the faces of the group around the table showed that they, too, felt the same.

At the beginning of September 1977, I was asked if I would take the messages from Maitreya publicly. On September 6th 1977, the first public message was given, at Friends House, Euston Road, "experimentally", to find out, I suppose, how I stood up to the demonstration of this kind of overshadowing and telepathy in public—a very different thing from the privacy of one's own group. These have continued until now. At the moment of going to press we have received eighty-five messages. These are conveyed by me to the audience; no trance or mediumship is involved, and the voice is mine, very obviously strengthened in power and altered in pitch by the overshadowing energy of Maitreya. They are transmitted simultaneously on all the astral and mental planes, while I supply the basic etheric-physical vibration for this to take place. From these subtle levels, the messages impress the minds and hearts of countless people, who are gradually made aware of the thoughts

21

and the Presence of the Christ. He releases in this way fragments of His Teaching, to prepare the climate of hope and expectancy which will ensure His being accepted and followed, quickly and gladly.

It is an enormous, and embarrassing, claim to have to make—that the Christ is giving messages through oneself. But if people can rid their minds of the idea of the Christ as some sort of spirit, sitting in "heaven" at God's right hand; if they can begin to see Him as indeed He is, as a real and living man (albeit a Divine man) who has never left the world; who descended, not from "heaven", but from His ancient retreat in the Himalayas, to complete the task He began in Palestine; as a great Master; an Adept and Yogi; as the chief actor in a Gospel Story which is essentially true, but much simpler than hitherto presented; if people can accept that possibility, then the claim to receive telepathic communications from such a closer and more knowable Being is also, perhaps, more acceptable. In any case, I leave it to a study of the quality of the Messages themselves to convince or otherwise. For many people, the energies, which flow during the overshadowing, convince. Many who come to these meetings are clairvoyant in various degrees, and their visions of the overshadowing as it takes place is for them the most convincing evidence of all.

Perhaps the above will help to explain why I speak of the Masters and the Christ and Their reappearance with conviction. For me, Their existence is a fact, known through my direct experience and contact. It is in the hope of awakening others to the reality of that fact, and to the further, momentous, fact of Their return now to the everyday world to lead us into the Aquarian Age, that this book is written.

BENJAMIN CREME

London 1979

THE REAPPEARANCE OF THE CHRIST AND THE MASTERS OF WISDOM

THIS INTRODUCTORY ESSAY, slightly revised to bring it up to date, was given as a paper at the New Themes for Education Conference, April 1977, held at Dartington Hall, Totnes, Devonshire, England, and is published here by kind permission of the Dartington Society.

There follows a selection of Questions and Answers recorded at regular public lectures since May 1975. At these lectures, since September 6th 1977, Maitreya, the Christ, has given a Message to the audience. Several of these are included. The method used is mental overshadowing (without trance) and the telepathic rapport which this makes possible.

Writing out of a background of the Alice Bailey Teachings with additional material arrived at through my own inner contacts and experiences, I make various prophetic statements which are, by their nature, impossible of immediate proof. While I am convinced of their truth, I make them in no spirit of dogmatic assertion.

The subject of a coming Avatar or World Teacher or Christ is one that has enthralled men of all backgrounds and teachings for centuries. Even the most skeptical will often express the wish that such a desirable event were possible, however unlikely. To these, this paper is presented as an interesting hypothesis. To those who do believe in the possibility of such an appearance, it is offered in the hope that they may find in it a deeper conviction and a definite basis in fact for their joyous anticipation.

INTRODUCTION

The Christ, the World Teacher, is now in the World, to inaugurate the New Age of Synthesis

WE ARE MOVING into a period of climax, leading to events which will fundamentally alter life as we know it. Tremendous changes are taking place in all departments of life, preparatory to the establishment of entirely new modes of social living and relationship, based on sharing and co-operation.

To some people, this portends the Second Coming of the Christ. To others it is the realisation that only through a profound inner change and readiness for a new direction in our political, economic and social life can humanity survive. Is it not possible that *both* of these approaches are correct?

There is a growing awareness that a new spiritual age is dawning, under the guidance of the Spiritual Hierarchy of Masters of the Wisdom. They are men who have gone ahead of us in evolution; who have perfected Themselves; whose energies and ideas have been the stimulating factors behind our evolution; and who are beginning to emerge from Their ancient retreats to guide us into the Aquarian Age.

They do not come alone. Under cyclic law, and in response to humanity's need, They are returning to outer work in the world with Their Head and Leader, The World Teacher, the One we in the West call the Christ.

We shall shortly realise that there lives among us now a man who embodies in Himself the hope and aspirations of the religious groups as well as the practical aspirations for a better life for all, of the political and economic thinkers.

On July 19th 1977, this Great One, Maitreya, the Christ, the Lord of Love Himself, entered His "point of focus" as it is called, a certain country in the modern world.

24

He will show humanity the steps which it should take to regenerate itself, and to create a civilisation based on sharing, co-operation and goodwill, leading inevitably to world brotherhood.

Soon we shall see this man of extraordinary qualities. Recognise Him by His spiritual potency; His wisdom and breadth of view; His inclusiveness and love; His grasp of human problems and ability to indicate the solutions to man's dilemma—political and economic; religious and social.

He is Divine, having perfected Himself and manifested the Divinity potential in each of us. He is a man too, and comes as a brother, teacher and friend, to inspire humanity to create for itself a better and happier world. To those who can respond He will show the way into that state of Being in which Reality, or God, is an ever-present experience, and of which joy and love are the expression.

The Spiritual Hierarchy and the New World Order

People have been led to leave the Churches in large numbers because the Churches have presented a picture of the Christ impossible for the majority of thinking people today to accept—as the One and Only Son of God, sacrificed by His Loving Father to save Humanity from the results of its sins; as a Blood Sacrifice straight out of the old and outworn Jewish Dispensation; as the unique revealer of God's nature, once and forever, never to be enlarged and expanded as man himself grows in awareness and ability to receive other revelations of that Divine nature; and as waiting in some mythical and unattractive Heaven until the end of the world, when He will return in a cloud of glory to the sound of Angels' trumpets, and, descending from these clouds, inherit His Kingdom.

The majority of thinking people today have rejected this view, but are left with no answers to the meaning of life and evolution or any clear idea of the way forward, or any sure faith in the *fact* of God or of His continuing contact with, and love for, mankind. The view put forward by esotericism is surely

25

more rational and acceptable and more in line with modern man's knowledge of history and science and of religions other than Christianity.

Esotericism might be described as the philosophy of the evolutionary process both in man and the lower kingdoms in nature. It is neither solely an art, nor a science; nor is it a religion, but partakes of something of all of these. It is the science of the accumulated Wisdom of the ages, but dynamic rather than academic in its application to our lives from day to day. It presents a systematic and comprehensive account of the energetic structure of the Universe and of man's place within it, and it describes the forces and influences that lie behind the phenomenal world. It is also the process of becoming aware of, and gradually mastering, these forces.

A growing number of people are no longer content to accept a purely material view of the world when all their experience points to the contrary. Higher states of consciousness and the control over matter which results have been demonstrated over and over again, in many ways and on many levels, from the great yogis of India to Yuri Geller.

The great and growing interest in Eastern philosophy and religion; in reincarnation or the law of rebirth; in the power of the mind over matter; in the etheric planes of matter, as evidenced in the work of Wilhelm Reich and in Kirlian Photography; in homoeopathy, acupuncture, spiritual healing and radionics; all this is direct evidence of our growing awareness of levels of being and knowing above the physical body and the concrete mind. This is part of a great shift in consciousness which is everywhere taking place, and a direct result of our sense that the old modes of thought and feeling are no longer adequate to express our growing awareness of Reality, thus revealing our readiness for a new Revelation.

There is no doubt of the new spiritual awakening which is everywhere taking place, which must eventually lead to an era of world brotherhood—the keynote of the coming age of Aquarius. What is happening now is the outcome of inner forces, which are effecting great changes in human thinking and consciousness. This will result in the complete reorganisation

26

of the world's institutions and social structures which no longer answer man's true needs.

Throughout the world the new approaches to reality are emerging, and the new values which should govern our life in the coming age are beginning to be defined. This will entail the reorganisation of our political, economic, and financial systems along more rational and just lines.

In the field of economics, the implementation of the principle of sharing the world's produce should be seen as the overriding priority, to change the present gulf which exists between the living standards of the West and those of large sections of the Third World, into a more equitable, and therefore more stable, situation. A direct effect of the mounting awareness of this need is the growing concern for the underprivileged peoples of the world and the growing determination of these same underprivileged to rectify their situation.

The financial changes needed must follow the logic of this more equitable distribution of the world's resources. A sophisticated form of barter based on an agreed value for each country's produce should be substituted for the present system, wherein a distorted value is placed on manufactured goods to the disadvantage of those countries whose main produce is natural commodities. Such a system would open the way for a healthier economic relationship to exist between nations at different stages of development.

The present political systems will presently be seen, each of them, to be in various stages of transition, and therefore not in themselves as mutually exclusive as they now appear. Greater world harmony will result.

The present and growing interest in environmental and ecological problems can be seen as the logical outcome of the gradual awareness in humanity that it is not a separate part of the planet but an integrated part of a greater Whole, which includes all the kingdoms in nature.

To many today, this awareness includes the recognition of higher states of consciousness attained by those who make up the emerging spiritual kingdom, the Masters and Initiates of the world. Their existence was first revealed in modern times by H. P. Blavatsky, co-founder of the Theosophical Society, as long ago as 1875. A more detailed communication about the Masters and Their work was given by Alice A. Bailey between 1919 and 1949. In her book, *The Externalisation of the Hierarchy*, she revealed the existence of a planned return to physical plane work and activity by this group of enlightened men, which return, I submit, has already begun.

It is evident that man has made a great advance from his primitive beginnings. Each civilisation and culture has seen humanity step forward a little further in the expression of its potential. Many believe that this evolutionary process has been guided for millennia according to a Plan by these more highly evolved men, known to esotericists as The Spiritual Hierarchy of Masters. The history of mankind can be seen as the response to the ideas released sequentially into the world by Them to bring about the advances in knowledge and wisdom, of which the creative arts, sciences, politics and religion are the expression.

All the great religions hold before humanity the idea of a further revelation which will be given by a future Teacher or Avatar. Christians hope for the Christ's return, the Buddhists look for the coming of another Buddha, the Lord Maitreya, while the Muslims await the coming of the Imam Mahdi, the Hindus, the Bodhisattva or Krishna, and the Jews the Messiah. Each of them expects a Coming One, a Revealer of new Truths and a Guide into the future.

Esotericists know them all as one Being, the World Teacher, the supreme Head of the Spiritual Hierarchy of Masters, and look for His imminent return now as we enter the Aquarian Age.

In every age Teachers have come forth from this spiritual centre to enable mankind to take its next evolutionary step; we know them, among others, as Hercules, Hermes, Rama, Mithra, Vyasa, Sankaracharya, Krishna, Buddha, and the Christ. All perfect men in their time, all sons of men who became Sons of God, for having revealed their innate Divinity.

They are the custodians of a Plan for the evolution of Humanity and the kingdoms of nature. This Plan works out through the agency of the esoteric Hierarchy of Masters who substand all world events and constitute the invisible (because unknown) government of the planet. The Masters of the Wisdom are those members of the human family who have made the evolutionary journey ahead of us; who, having perfected themselves, by the same steps by which we advance, have accepted the responsibility of guiding the rest of us to that same achievement. They (or Their predecessors) have been behind the whole evolutionary process, guiding and helping man, through a gradual expansion of consciousness, to reveal sequentially, his innate Divinity, and to become, like Them, Divine, perfected or illumined Beings.

The esoteric process known as Initiation is the scientific path to this perfectionment, whereby man becomes united and at-one with his Source. This path of perfectionment is marked off by five major steps or points of crisis and tension. Each initiation results in a tremendous expansion of awareness or consciousness which brings an ever-deepening and more inclusive vision and knowledge of the true nature of reality.

No Master of the fifth Initiation needs any further incarnational experience on Earth. His decision to remain on Earth is conditioned by His desire to serve the Plan and not by personal Karma.

There is reason to believe that many (if not all) of the great figures in human history, were conscious initiates of some degree—for example: Pythagoras, Socrates, and Plato; Shakespeare, Dante, and Bacon; Leonardo, Paracelsus, and Mozart; Asoka, Benjamin Franklin, and Abraham Lincoln. All demonstrate in their lives or writings a knowledge of other and higher levels of consciousness, an awareness of the world of meaning and sense of inner synthesis.

The mysterious figure of the Comte de St. Germain, openly acknowledged as a master and an adept by all the courts of 18th-century Europe, is one of the few Masters of Wisdom to live outwardly in the everyday world, but letters from some of the Masters, those behind the formation of the Theosophical Society, reside now in the British Museum. Some of these were displayed in November 1975 in celebration of that society's centenary.

The vast majority of these illumined men live in the remote mountains and desert areas of the world, contacting the world but seldom, and doing Their work through Their disciples by telepathic communication.

In the esoteric tradition, the Christ is not the name of an individual but of an Office in the Hierarchy. The present holder of that Office, the Lord Maitreya, has held it for 2,600 years, and manifested in Palestine through His Disciple, Jesus, by the occult method of overshadowing, the most frequent form used for the manifestation of Avatars. He has never left the world, but for 2,000 years has waited and planned for this immediate future time, training His Disciples, and preparing Himself for the awesome task which awaits Him. He has made it known that this time, He Himself will come.

The Re-emergence of the Hierarchy

At this point when the Aquarian Age is dawning, the Masters of the Hierarchy are now ready to return, for the first time in countless thousands of years, to the everyday world, to inaugurate the new age of Synthesis and Brotherhood. Under Their great leader, the Master of all the Masters, the World Teacher, the one known in the West as the Christ, the esoteric Hierarchy will walk openly among us and lead us into the Aquarian experience. They stand now, waiting for us to take, of our own free will, the needed first steps in the direction of unity, co-operation and fusion. Then They will emerge with the Christ at Their Head, and Their Presence in the world will be an established fact.

In speaking about the re-emergence of the Hierarchy, one is speaking about an event which is scheduled to take place over some thirty years. It is not a sudden event, nor does it take place without due preparation being made. In fact, the preparations for this event started in the year 1425, from which time all other activities of the Hierarchy have been seen as being in relation to this unprecedented and momentous happening.

It means that the Planetary Hierarchy of Masters, Who have

worked on the higher mental planes for all these thousands of years, have reached a point in Their own evolutionary development which necessitates a re-enaction, this time in group formation, of physical plane life experience. This is the fundamental reason behind the planned and imminent re-emergence. The benefits which this re-emergence will confer on Humanity are not incidental, but of secondary importance. The Hierarchy of Masters must once again, only now as a Group, show symbolically Their ability to function on all planes simultaneously. This will be for Them the rounding-out of Their Earth experience, preparatory to Their embarking on one or other of the Seven Ways of the Higher Evolution. These are:

1. The Path of Earth Service
2. The Path of Magnetic Work
3. The Path of training for Planetary Logoi
4. The Path to Sirius
5. The Ray Path
6. The Path the Logos Himself is on.
7. The Path of Absolute Sonship.

We can know nothing as yet of this Higher Way, but the above tabulation may present to our imagination the scope of evolutionary development which awaits man.

The Christ's Decision

There are three spiritual festivals held each year by the Hierarchy. There is the festival of Easter, at the full moon in Aries, usually in April; the festival of Wesak, of the Buddha, at the full moon in Taurus, in May; and the festival of the Christ as the Representative of Humanity at the full moon in June.

At this festival in June 1945, the World Teacher, the One we call the Christ, announced His decision to return again to the world, if humanity, of its own free will, would take steps to put its own house in order. The conditions which He set were these:

That a measure of peace should be restored in the world;

That the principle of Sharing should be in process of controlling economic affairs;

That the energy of goodwill should be manifesting, and leading to the implementation of right human relationships;

That the political and religious organisations throughout the world should be releasing their followers from authoritarian supervision over their beliefs and thinking.

And when men's minds were moving in these directions He would, without fail, return at the earliest possible moment. My submission is that this moment has now arrived.

The decision of the Christ to return to *open* manifestation resulted in certain important happenings:

1. He used for the first time a great and ancient Mantram or prayer and gave it out to the world. In a form that we can use and understand, it is known today at the Great Invocation. It is given to humanity as a potent technique whereby the energies of Hierarchy can be invoked to bring about the necessary changes. It is now used by several millions throughout the world.

2. Two great Cosmic Entities now add their tremendous Energies to that of the Christ: the Spirit of Peace or of Equilibrium has again descended on Him and overshadowed Him in a manner similar to the way the Christ overshadowed and worked through the Disciple Jesus in Palestine.

   The Avatar of Synthesis, invoked by Hierarchy, brings into our world a great fourfold energy, gradually producing fusion and oneness out of the present separation. They stand behind Him and augment His power tremendously.

The New Group of World Servers

To prepare the way for the Christ, a new group has been formed in the world. Subjectively linked to Hierarchy, they form a vanguard through whom He can work. They have no outer organisation but can be found in every country without exception.

Any moment now the world will see the emergence of men and women of ability and insight who have within themselves the answers to the problems which beset the world today. They also have at heart the good of all. They stand ready to engage themselves in the task of reorganisation of the world's social structure along more spiritual lines when called upon to do so. This will shortly be the case.

The Masters will train them in their specific tasks and supply the needed energetic stimulus.

Their names are known to few but their coming influence in world affairs will be great. They will set in motion the changes, which, gathering momentum, will transform the world.

Already certain Masters are making forays into the world from Their retreats, for short acclimatising periods. During 1976, in five major spiritual centres or outlets—New York, London, Geneva, Darjeeling, and Tokyo—a Master appeared. He is gathering together His co-workers in the various groups; He co-ordinates and stimulates the activities of these groups, and, in ever-widening circles, the radiance of these five centres will spread across the world, preparing men everywhere for the Christ's Presence. A great wave of spiritual expectancy will sweep across the planet, and on that wave the Christ will make His appearance.

From these existing groups in all fields of work—political, religious, social, scientific, educational and cultural—will be formed a nucleus who will be trained directly by the Master Himself. Gradually they will be called upon for help and advice by governmental agencies, and their effective power to influence governmental decisions will increase. They can thus directly lay the foundations of the new world order.

The next one to two years will see this growth of power and effectiveness in the world. Administrative and governmental positions will be offered to certain members of the inner group who can then directly implement the needed changes. In this way, a gradual transformation of society will be made without the disorder and traumatic effects of the usual political revolutions as, for instance, in the Cultural Revolution in China, and its counterparts in Africa and South America. Far-reaching changes will be made with the minimum disruption of the existing social fabric, and this in a logical and orderly fashion, through legislation and general agreement. The democratic principle will still hold, and will be seen to be effective when truly directed to the common good. The participation of all sections of society in the construction of the new social order will ensure the speedy adoption of the measures necessary for its implementation.

There is no doubt that there will be opposition from those more privileged members of society who will see, in the changes which must ensue, a loss of their traditional status and power; but the need for change will become so overwhelmingly obvious, that they will find themselves increasingly powerless to stop the momentum. The present caste system has to go, in the interests of the One Humanity.

The incredibly powerful international banking and financial institutions will prove to be among the last to accept the fact that a complete change in the world's financial and economic order is imperative. To meet this obstacle, the Hierarchy has plans already made and ready to be put into effect. These involve the reconstruction of the world financial and economic order. A group of high Initiates, themselves economists, industrialists, and financial experts of great experience and achievement, are working with the Hierarchy, and have evolved a series of blueprints, alternative inter-related plans, which will solve the redistribution problems which are at the basis of the present world crisis. These can and will be speedily implemented when the need is seen and accepted, which acceptance will be forced on the united nations of the world by the weight of a now informed public opinion. The cry for help and justice from the poor and starving nations will be too loud and too dramatic to ignore. The stage will then be set for the Christ to make known His Presence and lead mankind into the Aquarian experience.

All this may seem to some to be impossibly visionary and unrealistic; but those of us whose task is to make this first, preparatory approach to the public will be followed by others with specialised knowledge and training in organisation and administration in the fields of finance, economics, industry, and science; before long, they will be in positions of power, democratically elected by reason of their obvious wisdom and selfless concern for the good of all. From these positions of responsible power they will build the framework of the new age social structures.

The peoples of the world are beginning to realise that their felt need for a fuller, better life can now, for the first time in history, become a reality, if they make the effort required to overcome the inertia which has held them down for centuries. Everywhere there are moves being made in this direction. For most people, this is a time of crisis and uncertainty, but behind the apparent chaos is emerging a new pattern, a new way of approach to life, which has in it the seeds of the new age civilisation whose keynotes will be co-operation and sharing, tolerance and goodwill. These qualities are already firmly planted in the minds and hearts of millions and will gradually manifest themselves more and more.

This time of trial and testing will slowly give way to an achieved integration. Humanity, the World Disciple, stands on the threshold of a new awareness of himself and his true purpose, which is to act as the sorting-house for the energies entering the planet, and to transmit these energies in a scientific manner to the lower kingdoms in nature. By doing this, man will become a co-worker with that Source of all manifestation which we call God.

By an act of will, man will one day call into being an aggregate of forces and forms through which his superior intelligence can manifest. These instruments and machines will take over from man the burden of production of the necessary artefacts of community life, and so free man himself for that deeper exploration of his own inner nature and potential which it is his destiny to reveal.

In this way man will come to know himself as the Divine Being he is.

Physical Appearance in the World

There are those who believe that the Christ will not appear in full physical Presence, but will simply pervade the world with His Spirit and Energy.

His spiritual Energy and Presence already pervades the entire world. This is but one of His three modes or phases of appearance.

By His overshadowing of the minds of the disciples, influencing them telepathically, His primary work on the mental plane is being made.

By the outflow of the Christ Principle or Consciousness—the energy of the Cosmic Christ which He embodies and anchors on the Earth for us—His second mode of appearance has long been under way, awakening men everywhere to the new Spiritual life which awaits humanity.

On July 19th 1977 He implemented the third phase—His direct physical Presence in the world.

He will be seen and known by all when He reveals that Presence to the waiting world. This will take place when enough people are responding to the Teaching and energies which are emanating from His undisclosed point of focus in the modern world; and when the new direction which humanity must take has already begun to be established. Men must desire these changes for themselves; and begin implementing them of their own free will—thus showing they are ready for the new Revelation and Teaching which He brings.

The Discovery of the Christ

Gradually, men will become aware that there exists among them a man Whose wisdom, love, broad inclusiveness, and the incisive mind which cuts through to the heart of every problem, is quite beyond the ordinary. They will gather round Him, those who respond, and begin to emanate something of that love and wisdom. Through them, He can work. *They* will change the world through His influence. In time, so many will have responded to this influence that He can safely reveal His true nature and status. Then the world will *know* that the Christ is here.

He does not come primarily as a religious leader, but will appeal to men and women of goodwill in every department of human living. He will speak to all men, as the World Teacher, and show that the spiritual life is normal and natural for man, and can be lived in every field of human activity, and not alone in the religious field. He will emphasise our inner connectedness as souls, identical with the one soul.

One day soon, men and women all over the world will gather round their radio and television sets to hear and see the Christ: to see His face, and to hear His words dropping silently into their minds—in their own language. In this way they will know that He is truly the Christ, the World Teacher; and in this way too, we will see repeated, only now on a world scale, the happenings of Pentecost; and in celebration of this event Pentecost will become a major festival of the New World Religion. Also in this way, the Christ will demonstrate the future ability of the race as a whole to communicate mentally, telepathically, over vast distances and at will.

His task, and that of His Disciples, the Masters of the Wisdom, will be to inaugurate the age of Reason, the age of Brotherhood, the age of Love, and so bring men into full conscious awareness of themselves as integral parts of the One Divine Life.

The Christ, Maitreya, has taken this momentous decision to return now, ahead of schedule, acting as the agent of Divine Intervention to mitigate the effects of certain disasters which would otherwise cause widespread hardship and suffering; above all, by speeding up the process of change through His direct Presence in the world, He seeks to save millions from death and misery through starvation, and to release from bondage those now languishing in the prisons of the world for the "crime" of independent thought.

Also, humanity's reaction to higher stimulus is, like everything else, cyclic in nature. We are now on an upward wave of response to the spiritual outflow and by entering the

37

world now the Christ can take advantage of this upward move while it lasts.

His body of manifestation, which He has been preparing and which must be equal to the strains imposed on it by living openly in the world, is now complete. The world will soon know that the Christ, Maitreya, the World Teacher, is among us.

Total belief that all of this is true is not essential. An open-minded acceptance of the *possibility* of the Christ's return now is the overriding necessity at the present time. This alone would release in humanity a renewed hope and a spiritual expectancy which would galvanise it into a much needed change of direction; and ensure a positive response to His Message and His Teaching when He reveals Himself.

THE GREAT INVOCATION

From the point of Light within the Mind of God
Let light stream forth into the minds of men.
Let Light descend on Earth.

From the point of Love within the Heart of God
Let love stream forth into the hearts of men.
May Christ return to Earth.

From the centre where the Will of God is known
Let purpose guide the little wills of men—
The purpose which the Masters know and serve.

From the centre which we call the race of men
Let the Plan of Love and Light work out.
And may it seal the door where evil dwells.

Let Light and Love and Power restore the Plan on Earth.

The Great Invocation, used by the Christ for the first time in June 1945, was released by Him to humanity to enable man himself to invoke the energies which would change our world, and make possible the return of the Christ and Hierarchy. This is not the form of it used by the Christ. He uses an ancient formula, seven mystic phrases long, in an ancient sacerdotal tongue. It has been translated (by Hierarchy) into terms which we can use and understand, and, translated into many languages, is used today in every country in the world.

It can be made even more potent. Used in triangular formation it becomes very potent. If you wish to work in this way, arrange with two friends to use the Invocation, aloud, daily. You need not be in the same town, or country, or say it at the same time of day. Simply say it when convenient for each one, and, linking-up mentally with the two other members, visualise a triangle of white light circulating above your heads and see it linked to a network of such triangles, covering the world.

Another way, which can be used in conjunction with the triangle, is the following:

When you say the first line: "From the point of Light . . .", visualise (or think of, if you cannot visualise Him) the Buddha, the Embodiment of Light or Wisdom on the Planet. Visualise Him sitting in the Lotus posture, saffron robe over one shoulder, hand raised in blessing, and see emanating from the heart centre, the ajna centre (between the eyebrows), and the upraised hand of the Buddha, a brilliant golden light. See this light enter the minds of men everywhere.

When you say the line: "Let Light descend on Earth", visualise the sun, the physical sun, and see emanating from it beams of white light. See this light enter and saturate the Earth.

When you say: "From the point of Love . . .", visualise the Christ (the Embodiment of Love) however you see Him. A good way is to see Him standing at the head of an inverted Y-shaped table, thus: λ , each arm of the λ of the same length. (That table exists in the world, and the Christ presides at it.) See Him standing, arms raised in blessing, and see emanating from the heart centre and the upraised hands of the Christ, a brilliant rose-coloured light (not red). Visualise this rose light enter the hearts of men everywhere.

When you say the line: "May Christ return to Earth", remember that this refers to the Hierarchy as a whole and not only to the Christ. He is the heart centre of the Hierarchy, and although He is now among us, the remainder of the Hierarchy (that part of it which will externalise slowly, over the years) still requires to be invoked, the magnetic conduit for Their descent has still to be maintained.

When you say: "From the centre where the Will of God is known", which is Shamballa, visualise a great sphere of white light. (You can place it, mentally, in the Gobi desert, where it is, on the two highest of the four etheric planes. One day, when mankind develops etheric vision which it will do in this coming age, this centre will be seen and known, as many other etheric centres will be seen and known.) Streaming from this

40

sphere of brilliant light visualise, again, beams of light entering the world, galvanising mankind into spiritual action.

Do this with focused thought and intention, your attention fixed on the ajna centre between the eyebrows. In this way you form a telepathic conduit between yourselves and Hierarchy. Through that conduit the energies thus invoked can flow. There is nothing better you can do for the world or yourselves, than channel these great spiritual potencies.

AUTHOR'S NOTE

THESE QUESTIONS ARE not arranged in chronological order. Readers are asked to note the date of each question and its answer. All questions before July 19, 1977 refer to His Coming; those after that date to His Presence.

LATEST INFORMATION

My latest information is that since April 3rd 1978, the gradual emergence of the Christ has proceeded. He is now an accepted (and much loved) member of a community of people in His Centre in the modern world. It is as their spokesman that He is now entering the final phase into more public teaching. The speed of this emergence will be determined by the creation of the necessary atmosphere of hope and expectation by those who accept the possibility of His Presence. In March, July, and again in September of this year (1979), He took part in public meetings, speaking to audiences understandably enthralled and moved by His address. These public appearances will continue, more and more frequently, until He gradually becomes known nationally in His "Point of Focus", and then, as the spokesman for all humanity, throughout the world.

May I appeal to all those who can accept on any level, either as fact or even as a possibility, that the information given in this book may be true, to play their part in helping to make it known, by all possible means, on the widest scale? In this way can be created the climate of expectancy into which He can the more quickly emerge and teach.

London, October 1979

DEFINITIONS

24/2/77

What do you mean by this word "occult"?

Occult simply means hidden. That which has been hidden or esoteric for a long period of time is occult. Occultism is the science of energy, but the hidden science of energy; the science of energy on the physical plane we call physics. There is occult physics, too. But occult simply means hidden; not black magic or anything like that. This connotation has been applied to anything that is hidden or occult—"the occult". There is no such thing as "the occult". There is simply that which is occult and that which is known exoterically—that which is not hidden.

5/7/77

It is a pity "occult" in our ordinary thinking has such a dark sort of meaning.

Yes, it is used in a very loose sense by the media as to do with black magic and witches and all that sort of thing. The word, occult, in esotericism, has a particular meaning: it means not only hidden, but from the technical angle, that which is to do with the manipulation of energies. There are two main paths in esotericism—the occult way and the mystic way. The occultist is the mystic who is also the scientist, the scientist of the energies, the practical mystic. Whereas the mystic is not necessarily the occultist. So it has a specific, technical meaning as well.

24/9/76

I just want you to define a word which I am a bit puzzled about. You juxtapose "mental" and "astral", and I had always thought of astral as something opposed to physical. Could you give me your definition?

We work, as human beings, largely on three planes, four if you like. These so-called planes are really *states of consciousness*. There is the mental plane, the state of consciousness of mental levels. There is the astral or emotional plane, the level of emotions, or the emotional state of consciousness. Then there is the physical, which is twofold: the dense physical and the etheric physical—which is still physical, but of finer matter—between the dense physical and the astral.

10/2/77

What is the difference between energy and force?

Energy is the free flow of energy. Force is that same energy after it has gone through an agency. So we receive energy and transmit force. Energy is untransformed, unconditioned except by its own qualities; but as soon as it goes through an agency that conditions it to some extent—it becomes force.

14/7/77

"Everything that is material in this world, is the spirit world solidified." I am still floundering as to what is meant by that.

It is true. There is an ancient occult axiom which says that there is nothing in the whole of the manifested universe but energy, in some relationship or other, some frequency or other. Modern science has proved that energy and matter are interchangeable, so modern science has come to the same conclusions as the ancient occult teaching about the nature of reality. This discovery of modern science is on a par with any great revelation which has come to us from the religious field. Christ said: "God is Love". This is a fact. It is an experiential fact for many people. "God is energy" is equally a fact. Love—what we call love—is a great energy, a great magnetic all-pervading energy.

Energy can be materialised. Sunlight is energy; sunlight materialised is what we call matter. Matter is an aspect of energy—it has to be. It is a question of the rate of vibration of the particles which make it up. Modern science has shown that this table—which looks a fairly solid job—at the same

44

time is made up of tiny particles of energy floating round a nucleus, and these are in a certain configuration which make it wood. In another configuration it would be metal. In another, a human body. But it is all energy. It is occultly and materially true.

THE CHRIST AND HIS REAPPEARANCE

1/2/77

Could you explain the relationship between the Disciple Jesus and the Christ?

The Disciple Jesus, Who is now the Master Jesus, was born in Palestine as a third degree Initiate. The five major Initiations which take one to Liberation have their symbolic enactment in the life of Jesus. That is what the Gospel story is really about. It is a very ancient story and has been presented to mankind again and again, in different forms, long before the time of Jesus.

He was, and still is, a Disciple of the Christ and made the great sacrifice of giving up His body for the use of the Christ. By the occult process of overshadowing, the Christ, Maitreya, took over and worked through the body of Jesus from the Baptism onwards.

In his next incarnation, as Apollonius of Tyana, Jesus became a Master. He lives now in a Syrian body which is some 600 years old, and has His base in Palestine. He has, in the last 2,000 years, worked in the closest relation to the Christ, saving His time and energy where possible, and has special work to do with the Christian Churches. He is one of the Masters Who will very shortly return to outer work in the world, taking over the Throne of St. Peter, in Rome. He will seek to transform the Christian Churches, in so far as they are flexible enough to respond correctly to the new reality which the return of the Christ and the Masters will create.

I am afraid that the Churches have gone very far away from the religion which the Christ inaugurated; which is to do with sharing, with love, with brotherhood and right relationship. But this monolithic institution has grown up in the name of that simple man and transformed His simple teaching into . . . well, you know what it has taught.

I was raised a Roman Catholic and these ideas about Christ aren't what I'm used to: how can there be such wide differences in our view of Christ?

To my way of thinking, the Christian Churches have released into the world a view of the Christ which is impossible for modern people to accept: as the one and only Son of God, sacrificed by a loving Father to save us from the results of our sins—a blood sacrifice, straight out of the old Jewish dispensation. We have rejected this view, we have left the Church in our millions, because it doesn't tally with our knowledge of history, of science, and of other religions.

The esoteric view, I submit, is more rational, more probable, and that is that Christ is a man. To my mind the Churches have over-emphasised the divinity of the Christ. He *is* divine, but in the way that you and I are divine—only He has manifested His divinity and we as yet have not. The idea of a Christ Who comes from the sky, from some mythical heaven; that the clouds are going to open and He is going to come down in a long white robe; to my mind all this is ludicrous. It does not tie up with our modern scientific knowledge, of human psychology, of the facts of nature and of other religions. I believe that in postulating this view of the Christ, the Churches have separated humanity from the Christ. They have made Him an impossibly remote figure, whereas He is an example—He should be an example—to mankind. But as a transcendent, divine figure, cut off from all mankind, as a God somewhere up there in heaven, He no longer serves as an example. The idea of Christ as a man, living now on the planet; as a great evolved Being, one of many such, the most evolved, but one of many—"the eldest in a great family of brothers"—makes it possible for us to realise that one day we shall be like Him. In fact, He said so. He said: "one day you will do greater things than I have done".

It may be very difficult for Christians to believe, but the Christ is evolving too, just as everything in cosmos evolves. He came before as the Avatar of Light and Love. He returns now as the Avatar of Light, Love, Wisdom and Will, because in the last

2,000 years He has come into a total at-one-ment with the Will of God, which He had not done before. This was the "Gethsemene experience". He realised that He could not accomplish His task by His will alone, but only from God's Will; that is really what the Gethsemene experience is about. In these last 2,000 years He has come into a knowledge of the Will of God. He comes now to release that energy of Will and an entirely new aspect of Divinity will be presented to mankind. This is the New Revelation. We have shown that we are ready because we are beginning to sense ourselves as One. From the point of view of Hierarchy Who see more clearly than we do what is really taking place, from the planes from which They see things, the first dim outlines of the New Way, the New Dispensation, are clearly visible—hence the possibility for the return of the Christ.

The Recognition of the Christ

14/2/78

How will we recognise the Christ?

Very soon now, *within two months* from now, the Christ will start to emerge in the country where He is and gradually begin His Teaching. How shall we recognise Him? How shall we be sure that the one we see is indeed the Christ? There are many men in the world today who are giving very sound instruction, very beautiful teachings, and some of them are claimed to be the Christ by their followers. We know there are, today, many people who claim to be the Christ or Maitreya; and we know, too, that there is a prophecy which says that before the Christ comes there will be many false Christs, false teachings about the Christ, and that: "if someone points to a man and says, 'that is the Christ, lo, here! or lo, there!' do not believe him".

No one will point to the *true* Christ and say: "that is the Christ". The recognition of the Christ is up to each one of us, individually. The Christ is the Embodiment of the energy we call the Christ Consciousness or Principle, the energy of the Cosmic Christ. It is released into the world for us by Maitreya, the Christ, and to the degree that it manifests in us, we will recognise Him.

He will show that our political and economic life has to make a complete change of direction and become the spiritual activity which essentially it is; that our educational systems, our science and culture, should, again, take on a new, spiritual, connotation. He will speak across the whole range of human activity, and it will be by the breadth of His Teaching, the universality of His viewpoint, that we may recognise Him; by His tremendous spiritual potency, His extraordinary aura of purity, sanctity; by His obvious love and capacity to serve; by all of these we may recognise Him.

Many people will follow the Christ without recognising Him, without even knowing He is in the world. But they will follow that man because they believe in what He is saying, in what He stands for: sharing and brotherhood, justice and freedom for all mankind. He will be the spokesman for a certain type of group thinking along these lines. Not the Preacher of old. He has said that many will be perhaps surprised at His appearance. He comes, not as the Head of the Christian, or any other church, for that matter. It may be that the orthodox Christian leaders will be among the last to recognise the Christ. He is not the one and only Son of God, but the friend and Elder Brother of Humanity.

One day, very soon now, when enough people are responding to His Presence and His energy, the Christ will allow Himself to be discovered. Those of us who know where He is will be allowed to point, not to Him, but to the country where He is, and turn the attention of the media on that country. He will acknowledge His true status and be invited to speak to the world through radio and television.

The radio and television networks of the world will be linked up, and He will make His appeal, His call, to mankind. *By mentally overshadowing all mankind simultaneously, He will come into telepathic rapport with all humanity everywhere, and we shall hear His words silently entering our minds, in our own language.* We

49

in this country shall hear Him in English, the French in French, the Russians in Russian, and so on. It is in this way that we shall know that He is *truly* the Christ. Thus will be repeated, only now on a world scale, what happened at Pentecost; and in celebration of this event, Pentecost will become one of the major festivals of the new world religion which the Christ will eventually inaugurate. Our response to His call will determine the future of the world.

4/4/78

For the benefit of those people who might be going out to other countries and cities or whatever, and want to stay in tune with events, could you go over again the stages of this emergence—like a teaching coming from a certain spot on the planet.

My information is that He is already beginning to emerge in His Centre—in what is called "the point of focus", the country where He is. His immediate environment will be the first to see Him, those who live near Him. He will become known to them, in a certain way, as a certain kind of marvellous man. Gradually they will draw around Him. He will become their spokesman. This will go out, as a radiation, a little further, and He will become more known through press, radio and television, until His face becomes known in the world. He will be the spokesman for groups who are thinking along certain lines, ideas which are shared by groups of people throughout the world.

The Christ has sent ahead His vanguard to prepare the way for Him. His vanguard has for many years been educating humanity with these ideas—the idea of sharing, of that principle governing our economic affairs; the idea of right relationship, of justice and freedom for all mankind. These ideas are deeply gripping humanity today. Some people are concerned only about freedom. Some are concerned about right relationships. Some are concerned about justice, and some are concerned about love. Certain groups are all for the freedom of the individual.

That is marvellous, but it is somewhat limited. Others are for the distribution of food and raw materials. That again is marvellous. Other groups are taking a more synthetic line. The Christ will be the spokesman for all these ways, on the broadest scale, showing the answers to the problems involved in all areas—on a universal level; exhibiting such love and such breadth of vision; a capacity to see into the minds of different types of men; and so simply, so utterly simply, in simple everyday terms, so that all men can understand. Look for that man. You will find that He will draw to Him from all over the world, men and women who share these beliefs. They will gather round Him and He will work through them. When enough people are responding to His teaching He will allow Himself to be discovered. They will go back to their countries and say that the Christ is in the world, and that you should look to that country from which a certain Teaching is emanating. This will draw the attention of the media of the world to that country, and hence to Him. He will acknowledge His true Status as the Christ and will be invited to speak to the world.

4/4/78

He will be a man with no known antecedents?

No known antecedents, no. But enough. Don't let me give you the wrong impression. The manifestation of Maitreya, the Christ, is so simple you wouldn't believe it. All is taken care of. The antecedents are not a problem.

10/1/78

You mean He will be seen before He reveals who He is?

Oh, yes, He will be seen in the world before He declares Himself as the Christ. He has said that first of all will go out His Teaching. An aspect of it is taking place tonight and at previous meetings here. Then will follow Himself, as He puts it, "in full vision". He has said—

"Many will see Me soon and know Me not.
Many will see Me soon and recognise Me.
They are My people. Be you one of them."

51

Will He take a public stand? You said some people will recognise Him. Will He become a public figure?

Yes, He will become a known spokesman; both the stimulus behind and the spokesman for, a certain type of group thinking, concerned with sharing, brotherhood, justice; covering the political, the economic, the social and also the philosophical, religious and scientific fields—across the whole gamut. It is really somebody talking across the whole range of human needs that you should look for. He will be the spokesman for that type of group thinking, of those who are enunciating the principles which have to govern our life in the new age: Sharing, Justice, Freedom, Co-operation, Goodwill.

These are the principles which we will come to realise are the principles of Aquarius. In one word you can call it synthesis, universality.

Day of Declaration

4/4/78

There has been a slight misunderstanding. Someone rang me today saying that he had heard you saying that the Christ would be seen within a week or two. But he didn't realise that wouldn't be the announcement of Himself.

No, He will not have declared Himself. Within the next few weeks He is emerging and will take His place as a man in the everyday world, known, gradually, in His immediate environment. How long that process will be I can't say; I don't know the speed of this. There is a tentative time—not a date—when it is hoped that He may well be able to declare Himself, if all goes according to plan. It can be brought forward, and this depends on us. Presumably, it can be put back too. If we, very quickly, make the correct response, then as quickly He could declare Himself. When enough people are responding to His Presence, His energy, His Teaching—and the teaching that will flow from Him through the groups—then it could be really a matter of months after His Emergence into full public teaching till He declares Himself. But I cannot say it *will* be that. All I can say is that it is relatively very soon indeed, if it is the time given to me.

Author's note, October 1979: During an interview for Dutch Radio in March this year, I was pressed by the reporter to be more specific about the date of Declaration. My Master allowed me to say: "within two to three years" from then.

Bodies of the Masters

6/9/77

What kind of bodies do the Masters use? Are they born in the usual way?

The Masters who have come into the world now have come in fully physical bodies. Two-thirds of the Masters today are in fully physical bodies.

What I want to know is, were They born the same as anybody else, or did They come into the world in a different way?

There are certain Masters Who are in the same body as They were when They took the Fifth Initiation, which takes Them into Mastery, so They have not taken on another body. There are other Masters Who have created what's called the "Mayavirupa"; this is a body of manifestation, created by an act of will. There are other Masters still, Who are in bodies which are born in the normal way, as children, and they've grown up, but as Masters. There are many different methods for the manifestation of a Master.

The normal method, or the most frequent, for the manifestation of an avatar, is to take over the body of a disciple, as happened with Jesus. The Christ took over the body of Jesus and manifested through it for the last three years. The Christ, Maitreya, remained in the Himalayas, but His consciousness, or some aspect of His consciousness, whatever was needed at that time, took over the body of the disciple Jesus and worked through Him for the last three years of His life. This time He has come Himself.

What happened to the consciousness of Jesus while He was overshadowed or taken over?

The body was that of Jesus. From the Baptism onwards, sometimes Jesus Himself was in it; sometimes Jesus *and* the Christ used it simultaneously; while at still other times the Christ alone manifested through it. The consciousness of Jesus became the observer of all that took place.

28/6/77

I wonder what makes you say that the Christ must come from the Himalayas?

Only because that is where He is and has been for thousands of years. This has been known to esotericists of many persuasions and teachings for hundreds of years. Many people have been to the Himalayas and have seen Him. He is not hidden away. He is in a remote valley, and those who have the right and the need to go there have been and have seen Him. The world of men, generally, does not know this fact. The Masters are in the remote areas: in the Himalayas, the Andes, the Gobi desert, the Carpathians. There are Masters in the Urals, the Rocky Mountains, in various desert and mountain regions of the world. On the border of Tibet and India, in the Himalayas, there is a great spiritual centre 17,500 ft. up, where the Christ has lived for 2,000 years and more. Long, long before that. It is from that centre that the great Avatars emerge. It is an esoteric fact which I cannot prove, but which will shortly become obvious.

30/8/77

Rudolf Steiner seems to say that the Christ would not come in a physical body. Were there changes made after that?

Yes. Rudolf Steiner died in 1925. The announcement of the

54

Christ's desire to return to the world was made in 1945. The decision to reappear was made earlier, but the *mode* of the reappearance was not determined. In fact, there were certain disciples in the world, initiates, who were being prepared, gradually overshadowed, whose vibrations were being heightened, whose physical makeup was being prepared as possible vehicles for the Christ. There were four of them; one of them we have all heard about. They were being groomed, as it were, as possible vehicles for the Christ—as Jesus was a vehicle for the Christ. Then the plan to use a vehicle was abandoned. What the Christ has done is laid aside His body of Light in which He has lived all the time in the Himalayas, and *created* His body of manifestation—the Mayavirupa.

Do you mean to say He has suddenly materialised a body and passed into it?

Materialised a body, yes. But not suddenly; over five to six years. And into that body His consciousness has entered.

How old as?

As an adult man. He is a fully adult, mature man.

Did He just sort of appear somewhere?

No; He came into the world by aeroplane and so fulfilled the prophecy of "coming in the clouds". On July 8th 1977 He descended from the Himalaya into the Indian sub-continent and went to one of the chief cities there. He had an acclimatisation period between July 8th and 18th, and then, on the 19th, entered a certain modern country by aeroplane. He is now an ordinary man in the world—an extraordinary, ordinary man.

The Mayavirupa

4/10/77

When the Christ and the Masters return will They incarnate in the normal way, as children, and grow up, taking the usual length of time, or will They materialise?

55

There are several ways in which the Masters can manifest Themselves. Some are born as babies, and grow up in the normal way; some are in the bodies in which They became Masters. Others create a body of manifestation.

Is this the type of body the Christ will use?

It is in such a body—a "mayavirupa"—that the Christ now appears. For several years the Christ has been building this body of manifestation, and He has built it in such a way that He can live at our level of vibration, in the physical world of everyday life, at the centre of world attention, leading mankind for the next 2,000 to 2,500 years. That body has to be basic enough and resilient enough to stand our vibration, and yet, at the same time, sensitive enough to bring in enough of His true spiritual stature to convince as the Christ, and to do His work as the Christ: to release the energy of the Spirit of Peace and the Avatar of Synthesis; the Buddha; the Cosmic Christ energy, His own love ray; the energy of the incoming Aquarian forces; the energy of Pisces—the sum total of all that. He is a tremendous avatar. There has never been an avatar so equipped energetically as the Christ is today, with the energies of Will, Love and Light, and the whole of this in a body that will be resistant enough to withstand the effect of our vibration.

Now He has solved this equation. It has taken some years to build this body and He has done it in an altogether unique way.

He could come into the world in His Body of Light, but to live at our level of vibration for the next 2,500 years, for the Age of Aquarius, in such a body, would be painful in the extreme, and it is doubtful if the work could be done. It is also doubtful if we could stand the strain of His closeness in that Body of Light. His contact with us would necessarily be restricted. So He has created the body of manifestation, the Mayavirupa.

How do the Masters create the "Mayavirupa"?

They bring together matter of the mental, astral, and etheric levels, enter Their consciousness into that, and precipitate it on to the physical plane. In every respect it is a solid, physical body but They can appear and disappear at will. If a Master wanted at this moment to come from the Himalayas, He could enter that door in a physical body, which we would all see as absolutely solid. You could shake hands with Him, He could sit down there. Ten minutes later He could disappear and be back in the Himalayas. That body is real. It is a created, but real body. It is simply not born in the ordinary way. It is such a body that the Christ has created for His manifestation.

30/8/77

Are any of the Masters in female bodies?

The time for that is not yet. All the Masters take a male body in Their last incarnation, and there are definite, energetic reasons why this should be so. A Master is a totally soul-infused personality. There is no such thing as sex—male or female—on the soul level. There is only polarity of energy—positive and negative polarities of one energy. The Masters have brought both of these into complete equilibrium, so, in a sense, They are neither men nor women. They take a male body for its energetic qualities. The relationship between spirit and matter on this planet at this time is such that They must anchor powerfully in the world the positive aspect of that energy, as a balance to the negative aspect as it expresses itself in matter. In about 350–400 years time, this will change. It is a gradual process, and that energy relationship between spirit and matter, as we term them, will change sufficiently to allow Masters to take female bodies too, which then They will.

28/6/77

How long will He stay?

He is coming as the Avatar for the Age, so one must presume that He will stay for 2,350 years approximately, which is the Age of Aquarius. Then His place will be taken by one of the Masters, a second ray Master, Who is well-known to esotericists, called the Master Koot Hoomi, K.H., Who is now being prepared to be the Christ for the Capricornian cycle. The Christ, Maitreya, will then go on to higher work, work we could know nothing about. He will have finished, for the time being, His work for humanity, which has lasted for thousands of years. He will return later, towards the close of this planet's evolutionary story, as the Cosmic Christ, when humanity as a whole has manifested in perfection the "Mystical Body of Christ". Through the perfection of mankind, when all men are perfected, the Mystic Body of Christ will be completed. Then the return of the Avatar at the end of the seventh, the final round, can take place. It will be the Christ Maitreya, the Cosmic Maitreya, Who will then return to inherit His Kingdom. It is to this that H. P. Blavatsky refers when she states that Maitreya will come in the seventh round of this earth.

5/3/76

You were speaking about the Christ speaking on the media, and He would be understood in all languages—did you have in mind the phenomenon of "glossalaria", "speaking in tongues", when one speaks in a language one does not know and everyone understands it?

No, not that, but I suppose everyone knows that all those who came from all corners of the Middle East and heard the Disciples at Pentecost could understand the Disciples, not because they were "speaking in tongues" (that is a distortion of the facts) but because of the *telepathic* connection brought about by the downflow of the Holy Spirit on the Disciples.

Oh, not actual physical speech? This person who addresses the world . . .?

. . . . will be heard *inwardly*, each will hear Him in his own language, as if He were speaking to them in their own language. This is the guarantee for humanity that all of us eventually will have this capacity for instantaneous transmission of thought from one side of the world to the other. The interchange will be on that level with people who have arrived at a certain point of evolutionary development. It is also the way we shall know that that One is *truly* the Christ.

At the moment the Masters use this technique to reach Their disciples in the world. They don't, on the whole, send letters.

Some letters have in fact been sent by the Masters of the Wisdom—the "Mahatma Letters" are a very famous case, at the formation of the Theosophical Society. They are very interesting letters indeed—but this was because the recipients did not have the telepathic development to receive directly. The Christ is the centre of a group of Masters, many of Whose names are known to us in the West, Who contact Their disciples in the world through this telepathic process. The Masters now impress the minds of thousands of people who are quite unaware of this fact. This New Group of World Servers of which I spoke, is actually made up of two groups. There is an inner nucleus, who are consciously connected with the Hierarchy and in telepathic rapport with Them. They work under direction from Hierarchy. There is another much larger group who are impressed; who are subjectively related to Hierarchy on the inner planes, who are not conscious of this on the outer level, but are open to impression by the Hierarchy.

Those two divisions in the New Group of World Servers—both of them are receiving but one is consciously aware that it is coming from the Masters and the other thinks "Ah ha! . . .

". . . I've had a great idea!" What I must do is this. I feel I must do this. I must. Yes.

They don't realise it's from the Master—so they think it's their own idea?

Exactly. Or *our* idea—a group idea. And it becomes then a group idea.

The history of humanity really can be seen as the history of man's response to certain great ideas which are put into the mind-belt, into the mind of humanity by the Hierarchy. So it has been down through all the ages.

But sometimes man thinks "it's my idea, or our idea". . .?

Mostly, he does.

. . . and other times he realises it is coming from a higher source?

Oh, the inspired ones know—the Blakes know it is from a

59

higher source, the Beethovens or the Mozarts, or the Leonardos, or the Joans of Arc or the Shakespeares, but the majority of men of goodwill are responding to ideas which emanate from the disciples of the Masters, whereas the disciples themselves are responding to impression directly from the Masters. This can be both conscious and unconscious.

The Christ Consciousness

1/2/77

What did St. Paul mean when he said: "Christ in you, the hope of glory"?

This is the Christ Consciousness, the Christ Principle. It is the evolutionary energy, *per se*, the energy of consciousness itself. This is now being born in mankind on a scale hitherto unknown. It is this which is bringing mankind as a whole towards the gates of Initiation, into Initiate consciousness, which is divine consciousness. The Masters are divine. They are human beings who have revealed Their innate, essential, divine consciousness. They have become Initiate. Initiate of the nature of God. Therefore, They are able to manifest That. This is brought about by the inflow and expression of the "Christ in us, the hope of glory".

The One we call the Christ, the One who holds the Office of the Christ, the Head of Hierarchy, embodies that energy, anchors it in the world. It has become focused in Him in an altogether new and more potent manner, temporarily, for the period of this human crisis. He releases it daily into the world and it is transforming humanity, working in men to produce the new spiritual vision. By "spiritual" I don't mean that people will necessarily join the churches, but that they will make right relations; bring about the brotherhood of man—which is a fact in nature, if we could but manifest it. It is through the expression of the Christ in us, the Christ Consciousness, the Christ Principle, that this takes place.

It is also that energy which will bring about in mankind what

60

is called Spiritual Recognition. Through that energy manifesting in their hearts, mankind as a whole can recognise the Christ. As it manifests in them they will say: "I will follow that man", because He stands for what it inspires in them. As it plays through us, it evokes our spiritual nature—more and more—which means we want right relationship. We demand it. We aspire towards it. It plays on our whole emotional and love nature, and in so doing it makes us want right relationships for all mankind. When the Christ calls for sharing and co-operation, when this Individual becomes known as the spokesman for the groups along these lines, mankind will recognise Him through having that energy in itself. He embodies it. They will respond to Him as it manifests through them.

5/5/76

Do you think that the last coming of the Christ transformed the world?

Yes, I do. The last coming of the Christ released into the world, for the first time on a world-wide scale, that great potency we call love. Mankind as a whole has not realised and manifested this love, but many great souls throughout the last 2,000 years have done so. Many have become Masters, or Initiates, as a result of this outflow of the Christ. This release of the Christ Consciousness, or the Christ Principle, 2,000 years ago, has brought humanity today to the point where a large section, some few millions of people, are now standing on the very threshold of the first initiation.

Mankind has not yet manifested the love principle on a large scale but in the last 2,000 years the spread of knowledge, of enlightenment, has been almost universal, culminating in our sophisticated modern science. Goodwill, the lowest aspect of love, is now enshrined in the hearts of countless millions. This is a direct result of the Christ's mission in Palestine. Humanity is beginning to see itself as One, as a Whole, which is an enormous evolutionary development, impossible without the Christ's appearance to inaugurate the Piscean Age, which is now ending.

The Sword of Cleavage

Can you say something about the effect of the Love energy of the Christ?

Love is a great impersonal energy, and released into the world by the Christ, its effect is twofold. It takes all of the Christ's skill in action to ensure its correct absorption, because while it can and does stimulate goodwill, at the same time it can stimulate the opposite of that, which is hatred. It is essentially impersonal. All men will feel, and do feel now, this energy—the good and the bad, the altruistic and the selfish; all of us feel and react to this energy in one way or another. A tremendous intensification of these qualities is taking place and will continue. This energy of Love is the Sword of Cleavage. A great polarisation will take place in humanity, between those who are ready to go forward with the Christ, into the future, on the only rational basis of sharing and co-operation for the good of all, creating right relationships; and those who are holding on to the old separatist ways, who are ready (though they wouldn't see it in these terms, it would be the inevitable result) to plunge the world into chaos, and war—a war which now could annihilate the planet.

Mankind will soon see that there is no alternative to sharing the produce of the world. Every other method has been tried and failed, and has led inevitably to war, suffering, degradation and misery. That is the choice which lies before humanity, and which the Christ will present. In pure black and white, mankind will now see, is now seeing, the alternatives: sharing, justice, right relationship—or annihilation. There *is* no alternative.

4/10/77

How can we be sure that He, the Christ, will not be rejected?

The answer, of course, is that we can't be sure. But it's up to *us* to make sure He is *not* rejected. We willingly must follow. His is the task to lead and guide, but we *willingly* must follow. Otherwise He can do nothing. His hands are tied by Law. The decision rests with humanity. Those were His words to us here two weeks ago. The decision is ours, but as I explained, we have no alternative but to go forward through sharing and co-operation, and this is what the Christ will teach. Humanity is now absolutely up against it. It is in an impasse and there is no way out; it is staring mankind in the face. So much so, that all the uneducated and most of the educated peoples of the world are now terrified of the future. They see ahead of them nothing but destruction of one kind or another: destruction through pollution, ecological destruction; through famine; destruction through over-population; through nuclear war; or a combination of all of them. There is no way out at all. The Christ comes with a set of proposals which entail a complete redirection of human thinking and feeling. If we follow these, we go forward. We can reject them. It's up to us. He said recently: "Many will accept Me, but not all. Nevertheless, My Army of Light will surely triumph." And a long time ago, He said: "The end is known from the beginning", and you can assume that, though one cannot say (I cannot say, with any authority), "Yes, He will not be rejected, this time. He will be accepted by mankind", I know that He has come at the earliest possible moment—but not too soon. There has been preparation going on for many years. The externalisation of the Hierarchy actually started as far back as 1860. Certain disciples came in, such as H. P. Blavatsky and others, who have been releasing to the world the New Age teachings. I don't mean just the occult teaching. I mean new ideas of philosophy, of politics, of economics, etc. Mankind is now adult, and is prepared in an altogether different way than before (when Christ came in Palestine). The Piscean experience, the spread of education throughout the world, modern communications, have made it possible for a Teacher to come and speak to a really adult world for the first time. So the hope is—and I would say the almost certain *fact* is—that mankind will not reject Him.

Author's note: In many of the Messages, since the above answer

63

was given, Maitreya Himself makes it clear that He is in no doubt about man's response. In Message No. 11, He says: "My heart tells me your answer, your choice, and is glad." In Message No. 65, He is explicit: "Therefore, My friends, have no fear that mankind will reject me. My Plans are safe in your hands." In Message No. 77: "I know that within men sits a Divine Being, Whose Plan it is that Love and Justice should triumph. This being so, the end is assured." In Message No. 78: "But, My friends, I know beforehand your answer and choice. Through your love—the love in your heart for your brothers—have no fear, My dear ones, you will choose correctly."

4/10/77

How will the proposals from the "New Christ" differ from the proposals that Jesus, the Christ, put forward?

Fundamentally, when He first begins His teaching, they won't differ all that much, except they will be much wider in scope. They will take in the political, economic, social, financial, educational, and the scientific areas too, and not just religious or philosophical lines. In recent centuries, the focus of the Christ and Hierarchy has shifted from the religious and philosophical fields to the political, economic and educational fields. Hence the world-wide growth of education, the great political ideologies, the great economic experimentation. All of this is under the stimulation of the Hierarchy. And so it is along these much wider lines that the Christ will speak. This is why He might not be recognised at first by many people who perhaps are looking for the Biblical Christ: for Jesus, with holes in His hands, and a long white robe, etc., speaking about Church matters, and so on.

Fundamentally, what He will say we already know—and accept to be true—which is that right human relationships are the basis of life. From moment to moment, by our thoughts and actions, we set into motion causes, the effects of which make our life what it is, for good or for ill. This is the great Law of Cause and Effect.

When we understand this Law and its relation to the Law of Rebirth, we will come to understand the need for harmlessness in all relationships. The rightness, the inevitability, the "commonsense-ness" of right relationship will be driven home to us.

This will be the nature of the teaching of the Christ. It is fundamentally what we all know, but He will reiterate it and show the way to implement it—*through sharing and co-operation on an international scale,* removing fear: the fear of hunger, the fear of war, the fear and the mistrust and the despair that hangs over millions of humanity today. This will cause a tremendous reorientation of human thinking, and make way for the establishment of right relationships.

30/8/77

How are millions and millions of people going to accept what we are discussing tonight?

They will follow the Christ. He has followers from every religion and no religion. He is coming as a World Teacher. But what He will teach in the first instance is something we all know and accept to be true: that right human relationships are fundamental; they are the basis of our life, and they have to govern it. We must share the produce of the world among all mankind so that in the future we will not have, as we have today, 450 million people starving to death—with a surplus of food in the world of 4 per cent. Mankind in the near future will not accept that blasphemy, that obscenity.

How is this just going to come in to millions—55 or 60 million people in this country or whatever it is, 200 million people in the States—how is it going to come through? You're giving us lots of drifts which are fantastic, confirming lots of people's thoughts, including my own—well, can you expand slightly on the form of communication, how will it come through?

The Christ will not be talking about the relationship between this planet, Sirius and the Great Bear! He will not mention it. He will be talking about the necessity to share the produce of the world; the necessity to transform the political systems in the world, so that tolerance and goodwill are the norm. We are beginning to realise that we are in a state of total impasse. Unless we change the political, economic and financial systems—the whole social pattern throughout the world—this planet will perish.

We have today the means of destroying all mankind at the touch of a button. That is the alternative to sharing and co-operation. There is no other way. This is what the Christ will show. Through radio and television He will reach millions with His message. And not only the Christ, but all those through whom He will work. And in response to His message millions throughout the world will form themselves into groups for the active promotion of goodwill. From being, at present, a minority, they will grow into an overwhelming majority, demanding an end to separation, hatred and injustice. The potency of hatred, mounting now to a climax, will be opposed by this active movement of Goodwill. The groups in the Five Centres, stimulated by the Master resident in each, will spread the radiance of the Christ's Message: Sharing, Justice, Co-operation, Goodwill—the keynotes of the New Age.

21/9/76

We've been talking a lot about politics and economics, which are all very materialistic, but is this what the Christ is all about?

Yes, indeed. Absolutely. It is indeed. It is not primarily as a religious leader that He is coming. You may look for Him rather as an educationalist in the widest sense of the word, advocating changes in our political, economic and social life. All of these are fundamentally spiritual. Spirituality does not refer to religious matters only. Everything that lifts men above their present level, whether on the physical, emotional, mental or intuitional level, is spiritual. We must broaden our concept of what is spiritual in order to recognise the Christ.

He comes to show that the spiritual life can be lived in every department of human living—not alone in the religious field; that the scientific path to God, about which He will teach, is wide enough and varied enough to accommodate all men. Everyone, in the future, will come to realise the spiritual basis of life, and will seek to give it expression in his work. And whereas today only the seer or the mystic knows the true meaning of reality, this will be the experience of all men, whatever their way. Not all men are religious; religion is a way, a specific way. The Christ will show that all of us can come to an awareness of the ways of God. He will show the path to that, the scientific path, the path of Initiation; and under the guidance and stimulus of the Christ and His Disciples we shall know God—truly know and see God, in this coming age. Large numbers of humanity will stand before the Hierophant, the Lord of the World Himself, and in doing so will see the Face of the Father, the Face of God. This is an occult fact and is the promise given by the Christ to the world. This will be His main function in the coming age—to lead humanity into the Spiritual Kingdom, the Kingdom of Souls, or the Kingdom of God— which already exists, and has always existed, as the Masters and Initiates of the Hierarchy. Under the guidance of the Christ all of us will enter that Kingdom. This is His mission, to establish the Kingdom of God, outwardly, in the world. He will fulfil that mission if we respond to the need of the time, which is the transformation of society along more spiritual and just lines.

26/4/77

I feel very uncomfortable with this idea that I am going to see Christ on television and hear His voice through the radio. I feel also very uncomfortable with the idea that He is going to be someone Who is part of the political and economic world. It is not at all my idea of a Spiritual Being.

It has been the tremendous triumph of the forces of evil that the churches throughout the centuries have been allowed to monopolise this idea of spirituality: what is to do with the church and religion is spiritual and everything else is not. This is a misunderstanding that the Christ will now correct. You may feel uncomfortable—I am sorry, but this is how it will be, how it must be. We must show our ability to become One with All, the whole of this planetary life: with our fellow beings; with the animal, vegetable and mineral kingdoms. We must stop exploiting the planet and misusing its resources; stop exploiting the lower kingdoms and misusing their life; show that this is One World, One Humanity, One Life. This is the destiny of mankind.

The function of mankind is to act as a transmitter of spiritual forces to the lower kingdoms and so act as co-workers with God. This is his true destiny. He cannot fulfil this if he relegates the spiritual life to one facet of it—the religious life. He can only do this when he manifests true spirituality in every facet of his life. This must include our political and economic and social life, the structures of which no longer answer our true needs and therefore must undergo change. The Christ will make this clear, and show the way to establish political and economic structures which will allow our spirituality to manifest.

7/2/78

Is there any reason why the country that He is now living in is not given out?

If I were to say He is in such and such a country, you would immediately put two and two together and say "Ah, that is the Christ", as soon as you see Him. Your right of Spiritual Recognition would have been infringed. You have to recognise the Christ—not because you know He is the Christ—but because of what He stands for. It is the Christ in you, the Christ Consciousness, which helps you to recognise the Christ, because you will want what He is advocating, what He is saying. You will want to see it implemented in the world—if this *is* what you want. Those who follow Him will see that in Him, and many may follow Him just as a political-economic-social educator, not as the Christ, not knowing He is the Christ.

Or even not believing that there is such a thing?

Without even believing that the Christ exists! I am sure this is true. I am sure many people will follow that man without even knowing that He is the Christ, or believing in the reality of the

Christ. But if they love their fellow men they will see the necessity to implement the changes that He is outlining.

7/2/78

What will the return of the Christ and the Masters mean for humanity?

In the first place if we accept and follow the Christ it will mean a tremendous release of anxiety and tension. A new hope for the future, and a new inspiration will be given to man. At the moment, mankind everywhere is filled with fear; it sees facing it destruction of all kinds: ecological, nuclear, starvation. The return of the Christ and the Hierarchy will show men that there is a way out of their problems, and that when we take the first steps and change the direction of our political, economic and social life, we have the possibility of building a civilisation greater and more spiritual than the world has known.

For the poor, undernourished and exploited masses of the world, the return of the Christ and Hierarchy will be the beginning of true living. For the first time in recorded history, the produce of the world will be shared among all men. For the advanced, developed nations of the West, that third of the world which today grabs, exploits and wastes most of the food, raw materials and the energy of the world, a new experience—the "wilderness experience"—will become necessary. We will have to learn to live more simply. But the Masters will show that it is possible to live a simpler life, a happier life, when the wherewithal of that life is shared with all men everywhere.

When the physical structures of human living are reconstructed, and the principles which should govern our life in Aquarius are understood and being implemented, the Christ will reveal to men an entirely new aspect of Reality, a New Revelation, which it is His mission to bring. The Ancient Mysteries will be restored, the Mystery Schools reopened, and a great expansion of man's awareness of himself and his purpose and destiny will become possible. "The waters of life" of Aquarius will flow from the Christ, and men will have that "life more abundantly" that He promised.

The principle of sharing is the key to this glorious future for humanity. When the world is truly One, when the produce of the world is shared among all men, the secrets of the Divine Science, held in custody for us by the Masters of the Wisdom, can safely be revealed, and through its agency man can create a civilisation such as the world has never seen. Man will come to realise himself as the Divine Being he is, and will express that Divinity in a new creativity and livingness, under the guidance of the Christ and the Masters.

THE MASTERS AND HIERARCHY

12/10/76

What is the chief role of the Hierarchy?

To develop self-consciousness in all beings, and consciousness in the lower kingdoms. To be an example for humanity, and to transmit the Will of the Planetary Logos. They prepare Their disciples for Initiation and provide them with a field of service. They also protect us from an excess of cosmic evil.

They are releasing energy of one kind or another into the world, all the time. They are the custodians of these energies, and release them in a scientific manner to bring about the changes in the evolution of the world. We respond to them well or badly, and our civilisations and our life in every respect are the outcome of our response. These energies make us what we are. They are making the new world. They are forming the Aquarian Age. We are at this moment, through our response to them, intuiting, feeling our way towards, apprehending, the kind of structures, the kind of civilisation, which the new age will exhibit. We are building it now.

14/6/77

Has every planet got a Hierarchy?

Indeed yes. There is Hierarchy throughout the system, in fact throughout Cosmos. Our Hierarchy was brought into this planet by the Lord of the World, about 17 million years ago, to oversee the development of early man, individualised about one million years earlier.

26/4/77

Is there a Hierarchy of the Black Lodge?

71

Yes, of course. There is nothing but Hierarchy in the whole of cosmos. All of us are at some step on a ladder from down there to infinity. It is a fact in nature. There are twelve Adepts of the Black Lodge, six oriental and six occidental, very advanced in intelligence but totally devoid of the Love aspect.

28/6/77

How many of the Masters are in etheric bodies?

Two-thirds of the Masters are now in dense physical bodies. The other third are in etheric physical bodies, which are still physical, of course. There are always sixty-three Masters connected with the human evolution, but there are many more Masters connected with the other evolutions. There are between 400 and 500 Adepts of the fourth Initiation in incarnation; between 2,000 and 3,000 Initiates of the third Initiation in the world. There are around 250,000 Initiates of the second Initiation and around 800,000 who have taken the first Initiation.

23/6/77

How is the Hierarchy organised now?

The Hierarchy is divided into three major groups on the three great lines of force, each one embodying, channelling, being influenced by, one or other of the three major aspects of Divinity that we know—the Will aspect, the Love/Wisdom aspect and the Intelligence aspect. The department under the Will aspect has as its Head, the Manu, the Perfected Man, the Exemplar for our race, the fifth root race. He is the perfect expression of our fifth root race in its completeness. The Manu (the second of two) of the fourth root race is also still on the planet, in China. He is the perfect expression of the Atlantean race and His work will be to gradually take the Atlantean aspect of humanity out of incarnation. This will gradually become synthesised into the fifth root race; it will have done its work.

At the head of the department under the Love/Wisdom aspect is the Bodhisattva, or World Teacher, the One we in the

West call the Christ. He is known in the East by other names: as the Lord Maitreya to the Buddhists, as the Bodhisattva to the Hindus, the Imam Mahdi to the Moslems, the Messiah to the Jews. Each of these names, religious terms, is the name of the Head of Hierarchy. His personal name is Maitreya.

At the head of the other department is the Lord of Civilisation, the Mahachohan. These three Great Lords, Aspects of God, for that is what They are, have together stimulated and overseen the development of mankind throughout the centuries by the transmission of energies, and the impression of men's minds with the ideas which embody these energies.

The Hierarchy has changed form, personnel, many times over the ages, as members of the human race became Initiate and then Masters, so that the Masters of the higher levels could go on to higher work. Many leave the dense physical planet and go on to higher spheres, or to higher planets, or even leave this system altogether. Some of the Masters, for instance, if They are on a certain line of work, go to Sirius.

Stemming from the department on the third aspect, that of the Lord of Civilisation, are four further groups, on the four secondary Rays of Attribute, thus making seven major groups or ashrams. Each of these has seven subsidiary ashrams, making forty-nine in all. Not all of these are complete at this time, both as to personnel and also as channels for energy.

22/3/78

Is there any danger of the Masters losing Their awareness when They come into the world?

No, no danger whatsoever. The Masters when They come into the world, make a great sacrifice. Let us not be in any doubt about that at all. It is an enormous sacrifice. The Masters are turned both ways. They are turned downward, if you like, towards humanity, the Centre where the Intelligence aspect of God manifests, a great centre of energy. Hierarchy is the Centre where the Love of God is expressed. There is a still higher centre than Hierarchy—Shamballa, the Centre where the Will of God is known, in which dwells the Lord of the

73

World Himself. As the Masters evolve, They do so by turning Themselves towards Shamballa. They are pure manifestations of Love and Wisdom, but They are becoming more and more imbued with the Will aspect of Deity, and not only the Love aspect. They do this by turning Their face, Their meditation, towards Shamballa. To come into the world—and a large group of Them, some two-thirds of Them, are coming into the world—means that They have to turn Their meditative gaze, Their attention, Their face, as it is called, from Shamballa to humanity, once again. This is a tremendous sacrifice for Them.

In order that They won't suffer too much—as you say, "lose Their awareness"—which in Their case would be of the Will aspect of Deity—there is a smaller group who will not externalise Themselves, will not come out into the world, but will remain occult. They have taken special training which allows Them to come to a deeper, more intense awareness of the Will aspect of God and through Them that aspect will be transmitted to Their Colleagues in the world—so that They will be kept *en rapport* with the Will of God and with Shamballa.

Shamballa

23/8/77

Could you give an outline of Shamballa, as you understand it?

Shamballa is a centre of energy, the major centre in the planet. It corresponds to the crown centre in the head in man, and from it and through it flows the energy we call Will. In fact, all the energies flow through Shamballa, but the specific energy which we call the Shamballa Force, is the energy of Will or Purpose, which embodies the Purpose or Plan of God—God being that great Being who ensouls this planet, and Who is reflected on the physical plane (because Shamballa is a physical centre, in etheric physical matter) as Sanat Kumara, the Eternal Youth.

23/8/77

Where is it located?

74

It is located in the Gobi Desert, on the two highest etheric planes. One day this will be seen and known, when mankind has developed etheric vision. It was set in place, we are told in the esoteric teachings, some $18\frac{1}{2}$ million years ago, when the Logos of our planet took physical manifestation on Shamballa as Sanat Kumara, the Lord of the World. Sanat Kumara is a youth, a young man, Who dwells on Shamballa, surrounded by His Kumaras, His Council, including the historical Buddha, Gautama.

The Christ has the right to be on that Council but He decided, shall we say, it is decided between the Christ and Sanat Kumara, the Lord of the World Himself, that the Christ as Head of Hierarchy remains in a physical body in the world. The Buddha is not in a dense physical body; He gave that up centuries ago, to be on Shamballa. (You don't have dense physical bodies on Shamballa, but etheric physical bodies.) The Lord of the World, known in the Bible as the "Ancient of Days", has many names: the "Youth of Endless Summers"; "The King"; "The One Initiator"; "The Great Sacrifice". He is the Initiator at the higher initiations, the Christ being the Hierophant at the first two initiations. He is the nearest aspect of God that we can know. He is our "Father", the personal God of Christians.

Externalisation of the Hierarchy

23/6/77

Can you say something on the externalisation of the Hierarchy?

Slowly, gradually, over the next twenty-five years, the Hierarchy will externalise itself. Not all, but most of the Masters, and many of Their Ashrams (the groups of disciples through whom They work, which are also centres of energy) will be externalised, known outwardly on the physical plane. It will be the aim of large sections of mankind to find their own line of energy, whatever ray they may be on, and gravitate to the Ashram which embodies that energy. There are seven major

Ashrams and forty-two subsidiary Ashrams, making up forty-nine altogether. They will not all be externalised but many will be, and most of the Masters. Many of the Initiates of the Hierarchy will work openly, outwardly, on the physical plane, known to all men. The Mystery Schools will be re-opened and men will go to them as they now go to University, to learn and to take the disciplines which will prepare them for Initiation, and so into the Hierarchy. This will become the aim of advanced humanity in this coming age.

23/3/78

At every quarter century, at the twenty-fifth and seventy-fifth year, there are Great Councils held by the Hierarchy. Major plans are laid for the next, sometimes, hundreds of years ahead, and also for the immediate twenty-five or fifty years. At the Great Council in 1425, the Hierarchy came into the awareness of the fact that They would have to return to the world. They have come to the end of a cycle in Their own evolution, quite apart from the human evolution, a cycle to do with Them as a group; in fact, as the next kingdom in nature.

23/3/78

The human kingdom is the Fourth Kingdom; the Masters and the Initiates of the Hierarchy make up the fifth, the emerging Spiritual Kingdom, the Kingdom of Souls. A Master is someone who has expanded His consciousness through all the planes to include the Spiritual one.

The Masters, senior members of the Hierarchy, have to re-enact symbolically, Their life experience, and show, now as a group (each one has done it individually) Their ability to function on all planes simultaneously, from the densest physical to the spiritual. It was in 1425 that the realisation that the time had come took place, and every move, every decision, made by Hierarchy since that time has been made in the light of the knowledge that eventually They would come out into the everyday world. Not only the Masters, this is the important thing; not only the Masters as individual men, but some of the Ashrams of the Masters will be openly manifesting on the physical plane. This is already beginning. There are certain groups working now in the world which are embryonic Ashrams of the Masters.

Many of the Masters will come in and you will then have the Ashrams working on the physical plane, openly in the world, and of course, at the same time. on the inner planes. It will be a double manifestation. At the moment it is only on the inner plane that the Ashrams exist.

People have very different ideas about how the Christ will. return. Some see Him returning in a blaze of glory at the latter days of the *world*—when the world is collapsing (why He should come then, I don't know). An Avatar comes at the end of every age; it is a cyclic event.

The coming of a Teacher has always taken place whenever humanity had reached a certain point in its evolution; needed some new spiritual guidance; some new energy; an outline of a new way which would lead it into a new, higher experience of itself and its meaning and purpose. Whenever cyclic change was taking place from one age to another; whenever a civilisation was crystallised and breaking up, making way for a new manifestation, a Teacher has come forth, always from the same source—Hierarchy. We know Them historically as Hercules, Hermes, Mithra, Rama, Vyasa, Sankaracharya, Krishna, Buddha, as well as the Christ. There have been greater ones and lesser ones. But at every period of history, when the need was greatest, when mankind needed stimulus, a Teacher of some level or other has come forth to show mankind the way.

In line with this law, at the end of the Piscean Age—at this transitional phase between the Piscean and the Aquarian Age—a Teacher has come forth. He is the World Teacher, the Head of Hierarchy, the Master of all the Masters, the "teacher alike of angels and of men" as St. Paul put it. It is His return into the world, at the head of His Disciples, the Masters of the Wisdom, which is now taking place. Nothing less than this is now happening on our planet; and it is, if you can believe it, a privilege to be in incarnation at this momentous time in human history—a time for which there is no precedent. Many Teachers have come into the world before and that has been momentous.

But never before, since Atlantean times, has there been the World Teacher, the Teacher for mankind, the Eldest Brother of the race, and at the same time, openly in the world, the Masters of the Hierarchy. This is the tremendous event which is now taking place.

Avatar of Synthesis

10/2/77

Who invoked the Avatar of Synthesis?

The Hierarchy Itself, meaning the Masters, the Initiates and the disciples in the world. In the 1940s, when He was invoked, it was not known whether it would be successful—whether it would be the Christ Himself who would come, or whether the Avatar—this greater Being—could also be invoked. It was successful; He was invoked, so that the whole process has been speeded up. If it had been the Christ alone—I am not being blasphemous in saying this, or disrespectful—the transformation would have been much more painful, and long drawn out. Because of the successful invocation of the Avatar, this whole process of the return of the Christ and Hierarchy, and what that means to humanity, has been speeded up tremendously. It is not alone the coming of the Christ, the man; it is the transformation of humanity, the transformation of our very nature and Being. That is really what it is about. This has speeded up enormously—made possible by the Avatar and the Spirit of Peace, and of course the Christ.

The Master D.K.

24/9/76

Has anyone met D.K.? Is He in a physical body or only spiritual?

Yes, indeed, He is in a physical body. He lives on the borders of Tibet and India and is known to a large number of disciples in various ways—by physical contact, by telepathic contact and by other ways.

5/3/76

You spoke about the Masters of the Wisdom having some influence on the astral and mental planes, and then later on you spoke about the Christ, the wonderful possibility of the Christ appearing on television, that is, the physical plane—so what are you dealing with, the astral and mental, or the externalisation on the physical?

When these five Masters come into the Five Centres, New York, London, Geneva, Darjeeling and Tokyo, They will work in the first place on the mental and astral planes. At the moment all the Masters are occult, esoteric. They are not in the world—They may be in physical bodies, many of Them are, but They don't work openly, outwardly, in the world. From an energetic point of view They are not in the world. Energetically, They work from the higher mental levels, from the Buddhic plane, in fact—the level of the Spiritual Intuition—so from a very high plane indeed. What will happen now—in a very short time from now—is that these five Masters coming into the Five Centres will bring the level from which They work down on to the lower mental and astral planes. At the moment They can reach and work through Their disciples in the world—this is how They have worked for countless thousands of years—those disciples who are open to impression on the higher mental planes, on the Buddhic or on the soul plane. When They come into the Five Centres, They will work directly on the lower mental and astral planes. They will then reach more people, those who are open to impression on these which are all relatively low levels, so that Their influence in each of these Five Centres will be tremendously powerful.

They will also work directly on the physical plane with an inner group drawn from the outer groups in these Centres. This inner nucleus will be trained in specific tasks to do with the reorganisation of our political, economic and social life in the Five Centres.

These five Masters and the Christ Himself will externalise

79

Themselves on the dense physical plane, as will the other Members of the Hierarchy in due course, but the energetic level of Their work will not be limited to the physical plane.

21/12/76

How is it that these Masters and the Christ have not been discovered and written about by journalists?

They have been discovered and written about, indeed, but not by journalists. People have seen the Christ and written about Him and the Masters. There are many books in the world which are available. Some, unfortunately, are already out of print. There is one by Macdonald-Bayne, which is out of print, called *Beyond the Himalayas*. It is many years since I read it, but there is a wonderful description of certain Masters. There are examples, for instance, in *The Teachings of the Masters of the Far East* by Baird Spalding, of descriptions of the Christ and the Masters, and the Buddha, as They are, as They exist. There are many such people who have seen the Christ. He is available to those people who have the right and the need to see Him. We don't have the right but there are those who do see Him and they have written about Him. The average journalist would tend not to be one with that right.

THE FIVE SPIRITUAL CENTRES

5/7/77

Could you explain more regarding the Five Centres?

New York is the centre of energy for North and South America, (the energies work through the groups existing in the centres). London acts as the centre for the distribution of this spiritual outflow throughout the British Commonwealth of Nations, and that takes in most of Africa. Geneva is the centre for the distribution of energies throughout Europe and Russia. Darjeeling acts in the same way in Asia, north and south. Tokyo is the centre for the distribution of energy throughout the Far East. So the whole of the world is actually the recipient of the energies distributed from these five major centres.

There are many minor centres. I mentioned two. One is Rome and the other is Moscow. Some centres are not even activated yet and will not be activated for, in some cases, thousands of years. But in other cases, as minor centres, they will become active as the groups within them become potently active within the next 50, 100, or 200 years.

In the case of Darjeeling, the major group source is of course, Delhi, but the energy is from Darjeeling. The growth of the huge populations in these five centres is a direct result of the magnetic drawing of people into the etheric centres which they are—they are actually activated centres on the etheric plane. They have been active in some cases for thousands of years. They are not all active in the same way. Some are more active and some less. Some more on the inner, and some more on the outer plane.

4/4/78

You say there are Masters in each of the Five Centres. So there is one in London—in the city itself?

81

On the outskirts of the city. One near New York, one in Geneva, one in Darjeeling, and one just outside Tokyo.

Are They in the public eye, at all?

No, but They are working with certain groups on the physical plane. The Masters are working on four levels. They are working from the level from which They normally work—the Buddhic level, but also They have brought the level of Their work right down on to the lower mental and astral planes. They are stimulating the minds of the groups in each of these Centres. I mean all the groups—the political, economic, financial, social, scientific, educational, cultural, religious—groups across the whole field are receiving this stimulus—to coordinate their work and bring it into a better alignment and so save energy; so that they are moving together rather than at cross purposes. And a greater synthesis *is* taking place between the groups. There is an active synthesis movement going on within the groups that I am aware of. There are many groups within what is broadly called the "new age" movement, in this country, and in America and elsewhere, who are very conscious of the need to work together and bring about this synthesis. They are doing it under stimulus.

Some may not even know why they are doing it, but they are aiming for synthesis. Also, links between the non-political and the political groups are being formed. That is the outer grouping—they are being stimulated mentally and astrally.

There is also an inner group who are being trained on the physical plane. They know the Masters and they work with Them. This is a group who have a certain inner development; who know the Plan; who know how the Plan can work out. They have experience in administration and organisation in economics and government, and so on, so that they can be trained in very specific tasks. It is through these trained individuals that the Plan will work out in the Five Centres. The outer groups are being stimulated without even knowing they are being stimulated. It is a mental and astral impression—they are not given messages, but generalised impressions. They have a great idea—"I think we should get together".

82

They are responding to the generalised stimulus of the Masters.

4/4/78

I was wondering if there was One in London?

That you could phone up? There is a Master in London, but you cannot phone Him up. He will soon be known but He won't declare Himself yet—none of the Masters will declare Themselves until the Christ declares Himself.

EFFECT ON EXISTING INSTITUTIONS

5/5/77

What will happen to the orthodox churches when the Christ declares Himself?

We are told by one of the teaching Masters, the Master D. K., Djwhal Khul, that the Master Jesus will, around 1980, take over the throne of St. Peter, and seek to transform the churches. If the Christian churches are flexible enough to the new teachings, the new ideas which the Christ will bring, that form will be kept because it is meaningful to some 900 million people throughout the world. It is a great stabiliser in the world. It plays an enormous role. And the church transformed—because it will have to be transformed through responding to the new teaching—will have mainly a teaching function. In fact the church is supposed to have a teaching and a healing function. It hasn't always done that. Through the churches much teaching and great healing will be done; and also, through the churches, through the Masonic tradition and certain esoteric groups, will come the process of Initiation. In this coming age millions of people will take the first and second Initiation through these three transformed and purified institutions.

5/7/77

Why bother to reform the Christian Church?

The thing is that the Christian churches, like the Buddhist churches, have millions and millions of adherents. I think there are something like 900 million people belonging, more or less fervently, to the Christian churches throughout the world. Nearly 1,000 million people. Just under a quarter of the world's population. And the same for the Buddhists—maybe 8 or 9 hundred million Buddhists.

84

The Master Jesus is going to reform the Christian churches. The Buddha is sending two disciples who will do the same thing for the Buddhist churches; not to preserve them into the Aquarian age, but for a certain time, because of the enormous number of people in the world for whom the rituals and form have a very real meaning and function. It is not only a mental concept, it has an actual energetic function. It is a great source of protection for millions of people today. Because of this, the churches—where they are flexible enough to the new ideas, the new teaching—will be held together, the structures will be held together.

In the Christian rituals are embodied occult energetic happenings: when you have a priest of a high enough calibre performing the communion service, there is a downflow of energy from the Christ, perhaps through the Master Jesus, sometimes direct from the Christ Himself, into the priest, into the communion wafer and into the communicants. This takes place time and time again. Today, the churches are the recipients of tremendous spiritual energy.

The Piscean civilisation is crumbling and the attitudes to religion are changing, but where the structure, the form, is sufficiently elastic and flexible to be used, it will be used while the people who are in it still need that formula.

5/5/77

When you say all the churches have to be reformed, that will surely include Judaism, Buddhism and all of them?

Indeed yes. The Christ came before in Palestine as a Jew to finish the Jewish Dispensation (which was already 3,000 years old and highly crystallised in its thought); and to introduce a new and more correct view of God as a God of Love, rather than as a vengeful tribal Deity. The Jews as a people have still to go through the Piscean experience and acknowledge the Revelation revealed in Palestine through Jesus as the Messiah. Buddhism too, is highly crystallised and will be reformed by two Initiate Disciples sent by the Buddha.

85

5/1/78

Do you feel that this will affect the various secret bodies, secret organisations, like the Masons, the Rosicrucians, and so on?

Very much so. Apart from the Aquarian energies, which are synthetic, leading towards a kind of standardisation (only, it will be a unity with diversity, an organic synthesis, not the imposed standardisation which you have in certain countries in the world today, but a true unity and brotherhood brought about by a unity of motive), the coming religion, in fact this coming age, will be dominated by the great energy which has been coming into the world since 1675 and is now really mounting in potency—the Seventh Ray of Ceremonial Order, or Magic, or Ritual, or Organisation. The Sixth Ray of Devotion dominated during the Piscean Age, and most people in incarnation today are Sixth Ray. All our structures: political and economic; occult and devotional bodies; our churches; everything is saturated with Sixth Ray energy and Sixth Ray modes of thinking, which creates a tendency to fanaticism and separation. It is the Ray of Abstract Idealism or Devotion. So that all structures—religious structures are of course included—are so strongly coloured by this ray that they are inevitably fanatically separate. It is the response to the ray energy which has made them separate.

Aquarius has been called "the implementing force of synthesis or universality", and will bring about synthesis, universality, in the world, as men respond more and more to its potency.

The same is largely true of the Seventh Ray, but it works in a different way, in that it relates the higher to the lower. It is the relating Ray—synthesising spirit and matter—bringing these two together. It grounds the higher spiritual ideas and energies on to the physical plane; so that what, in the Piscean Age, has been an abstract ideal, will become a fact on the physical plane. Brotherhood, love, sharing, co-operation—all the ideals which people have had for centuries—will be implemented. There will be a greater unification, greater synthesis.

There are seven types of men, governed by their ray energies. There are never more than four energies in incarnation at any one time, so that largely there are four different types of men and women in incarnation. As souls, all men and women at the Third Initiation—even if they were on the Fourth, Fifth, Sixth or Seventh Ray before—have to find their correspondence on one of the first three rays—the rays of aspect. Inevitably, these three rays dominate and create all that we know. The four rays of quality or attribute, come out of the rays of aspect. There are basically three approaches to life.

The new religion will manifest, for instance, through organisations like Masonry. In Freemasonry is embedded the core or the secret heart of the occult Mysteries—wrapped up in number, metaphor and symbol. When these are purified of the extraneous accretions which have crept in over the last 7,000 years, these will be seen to be a true occult heritage. Through the Orders of Masonry, the Initiatory Path will be trodden and Initiation will be taken along the First Ray line of Power. Within the purified Churches, the Initiatory Path will be trodden and Initiation will be taken along the second line of Love-Wisdom. Within the esoteric teaching bodies of the world will be taken the Initiatory experience along the third line. So there will be three distinct outlets and areas of experience for the three major groupings of men. Of course, there is the One Truth; it is simply that for different types of men there are different paths; and what Christ said in one of the first Messages, giving His reasons for returning to the world, is relevant here: "I come to show you the way to God, back to your Source. To show you that the way to God is a simple path which all men can tread." It is a path which is wide enough for all men to tread. It is not simply of a religious nature, but no matter what area, or department of life a man is in, within that department he can express his awareness of the presence of God, give that expression, and enter the Initiatory Path in one of these three major ways.

The New World Religion

27/1/76

Do you see any role for the present religious systems and their monuments, in the new age?

Those systems which have the ability to change in response to the pressures of the energies and ideas and ideals of the time will have a place. But eventually a new world religion will be inaugurated which will be a fusion and synthesis of the approach of the East and the approach of the West. The Christ will bring together, not simply Christianity and Buddhism, but the concept of God transcendent—outside of His creation—and also the concept of God immanent in all creation—in man and all creation.

It will be seen to be possible to hold both approaches at one and the same time, and they will be brought together in a new scientific religion based on the Mysteries; on Initiation; on Invocation—the approach to Deity through invocation—and The Great Invocation will be used throughout the world, as it is used now by millions of people. It is planned that one day this will be a world prayer, and that the Three Great Festivals—the Easter Festival; the Wesak Festival, one month later; and the Christ Festival, one month later still—will be held simultaneously throughout the world; also the nine important, but rather less important, festivals at the nine other full moons throughout the year. These three festivals will be central to the New World Religion and will constitute, each of them, a great Approach to Deity—the evocation of the Divine Light, Divine Love, and Divine Will, which can then be anchored on the earth and utilised by man.

5/7/77

You said the New World Religion would be a scientific one—I don't think I like the sound of that.

By that I don't mean a very austere, clinical type of religion—cold and heartless—not at all. I mean scientific in the sense of *knowledgeable* about the purpose and meaning of the religion—about the energies which mankind will invoke. For instance, the practice of invocation will take the place of prayer and worship as we use it today.

The very heart and core of the new world religion will be the esoteric process of Initiation. The first two Initiations will take place outwardly, openly, on the physical plane, in the temples of the time—as the most sacred ceremonies of the new religion. It is a very scientific process, the process of Initiation, of which the Christ and the Hierarchy are the custodians. Through it, mankind will gradually enter into the Hierarchy. At the end of this age all of mankind will be in the Hierarchy—the "Kingdom of God", which is the Hierarchy, will be openly manifest in the world. The next kingdom up, the Kingdom of Souls or the Spiritual Kingdom is already here, as the Hierarchy. But the Hierarchy and humanity will gradually become One as a result of the Initiatory process. Gradually, Christianity, Buddhism and other religions will wither away—slowly, as the people die out of them, as the new religion gains its adherents and exponents, and is gradually built by humanity. In the meantime—and always the new is built on the essential structure of the old, where this is flexible enough to respond to the incoming energies—in the meantime, a revitalised Christianity and Buddhism will continue.

THE THREE SPRING FESTIVALS

17/5/77

The Festival of the Christ in Gemini—what happens?

The full moon in Gemini—the Festival of the Christ. This is a festival to celebrate the approach of humanity to God. In the New World Religion there will be a great unified approach to Deity, at all the full moons, especially at the Three Major Spiritual Festivals of April, May and June—Aries, Taurus and Gemini. Throughout the world these festivals will be held simultaneously. You can imagine what the accumulated effect of that Approach will be. Humanity will be taught, by the disciples, the great science of invocation which will take the place of worship and prayer as we know it today, and a united invocation of Deity will take place. A great Approach will come from Deity to humanity. By this very scientific process of invocation, the new religion will bring mankind, through the Initiatory process, closer and closer to the Divine Mind. Initiation provides an insight into the mind of God—gradually more and more of the nature of Divinity is released by the Initiate.

The Festival in June, the Festival of Gemini, will be above all the festival of Humanity. It is called the Christ Festival today because it is the Festival of the Christ as the Eldest in a great family of brothers; not only the Christ of Hierarchy, but the Christ as the Representative of Humanity. It will be, above all, the Festival of Good will; the shared Will-to-good of humanity, which we express as Goodwill.

This is the next aspect of divinity to be manifested by humanity—goodwill is an aspect of the love nature of God and our next step in the expression of that nature. It is part of the Plan of God that we manifest this goodwill, this love nature, and as we bring our own little personal, separate will into line with the Divine Will, it becomes possible for the Will of God to manifest truly for the first time on earth. This is what a true spiritual age is about. A spiritual age is the outcome of the manifestation of God's Will on Earth.

17/5/77

Where do these Festivals take place?

In the secret valleys of the Hierarchy, but even today, humanity is beginning to grow into the awareness of the rituals of the New World Religion. All over the world, groups are meeting at the times of the full moon—especially at the three major festivals, but also at the nine minor full moon festivals—to tune into the energies which are uniquely available at these times. At each full moon there is a unique energy which conditions all the other energies normally flowing then. Above all, at the Three Spiritual Festivals, certain great divine energies become available: the energies of Light, of Love, of Will. Groups today are learning, through invocation and meditation, to tune into, anchor on earth, and transmit, the energies streaming from outer galaxies and from the zodiac, which are available at these specific times. In many parts of the world there are such groups learning the rudiments, as it were, of the structure of the new world religion, which will be a very scientific religion, based on the science of invocation; on the science of that process we call Initiation; and it will be characterised by a great inclusiveness. It will be world wide.

The Christ will bring together, in the New World Religion, the approaches of the East and the West which today are separate. They are apparently contradictory, but in fact are complementary. That is, the approach to God as transcendent, above and outside of His creation, uncontactable by His creation; and the approach to God as immanent in all nature; in man and all Being.

In this way we shall realise that there is no one, no person and nothing, through whom God does not manifest at some level. Hence the *fact* of brotherhood. Brotherhood is a *fact* in nature. We are all part of One Life. We are all children of God, each one of us. We have to manifest this. We know this. Theoretically we accept this—we pay lip-service to it—but we don't actually manifest it. We don't act as if all men were brothers.

At the moment 450 million of our brothers are starving to death in a world of plenty, in a world in which there is a surplus of food. This is the opposite of the truth of brotherhood. If we were manifesting the true brotherhood of mankind, the true divinity in mankind, then we would not have this blasphemy.

The Wesak Festival

8/10/76

What exactly is going on in the Wesak Valley?

Wesak is the name of the Festival, the Festival of the Buddha, which Hierarchy holds in a valley in the Himalayas. It is also held all over the Eastern world, exoterically, in May.

What is going on generally in that valley?

Right at this moment, I really don't know, but at the Wesak Festival I can tell you roughly what takes place: all the members of the Hierarchy gather together—both in the physical body and out of the physical—in this valley. The Christ and Heads of the other two great Departments—the Department of the Manu and the Department of the Lord of Civilisation—these three Great Lords, stand in triangular formation in front of an enormous flat stone on which stands a large crystal bowl, filled with pure water. When the moon rises above the horizon, at that moment of the full moon in Taurus, the Buddha comes. Gautama Buddha comes from Shamballa and hovers over the stone, over the crystal bowl, and transmits to the Christ the energy which is called the Shamballa Force—the great First Ray of Will or Power. He will transmit it to the Christ every year, in ever-mounting potency, until the year 2,000. It is circulated by the Christ through the Three Lords (Himself, the Manu and the Lord of Civilisation), held by Hierarchy, and then gradually released to the world until the full moon in Libra, when it is withdrawn until the following Wesak. The locals come there, the Tibetans, and the pilgrims from Northern India, and gather at one end of the valley while this great ceremony is taking place. Then the water in the crystal bowl which is blessed by the Presence of the Buddha, is shared out among all those participating. It is a deeply significant esoteric event.

24/5/77

Why are the festivals held at the time of the full moon?

Because at the time of the full moon the energies are more available. There is opened an energetic conduit which makes them more potent and more available—it is not a question that the energies are only potent as those times, but for mankind it is the time of greatest assimilation. Mankind finds the time of the full moon easier to tune into, align itself with, and assimilate these energies.

The Master D.K. has said that it is as if a door is opened between the sun and the moon which makes events of a spiritual nature possible. The moon is always there, but when the moon is full in relation to earth then this conduit is most open, which relates humanity to the Hierarchy more easily than at other times.

The moon is a dead planet—it has no life of its own, no light of its own, only reflected light. But from the moon streams an energy, both mental and astral, which is the build-up, the accumulated thought-form, from the time when mankind lived on the moon and populated the earth from the moon. The moon has since become extinct and the sooner it is out of our system the better. It is a malefic carcass, from the occult point of view.

The Turin Shroud

28/3/78

Could you please tell us something about the Turin shroud and whether it is authentic or not?

I personally believe that it is absolutely authentic, that it is the shroud in which the body of Jesus was wrapped after the crucifixion. The image on it was deposited intentionally and left there for future generations to hold to the reality of resurrection, because that is what the whole gospel story is about. The gospel story is not about crucifixion. It is about resurrection.

It is most interesting that the greatest authentication of the shroud which has been produced just recently by scientific means, has come a few months after the Christ came into the world. This is one of the signs. The Christ said in Message No. 10: "I come to tell you that you will see Me very soon, each in his own way. Those who look for Me in terms of My beloved Disciple, the Master Jesus, will find His qualities in Me. Those who look for Me as a Teacher are nearer the mark, for that is what I am. Those who search for signs will find them, but My method of manifestation is more simple." The coming of the Christ last year does not depend on signs, like the Shroud and various other signs, but they are part of the signs which are showing humanity that something quite extraordinary is happening at this time, and restoring not just the faith of the Christians, but the hope of mankind.

The hope of mankind is the hope of resurrection, fundamentally; and the gospel story is really the re-enactment of a story which has been presented to humanity again and again, through all the ages—the story of Initiation.

The Birth at Bethlehem symbolises the first Initiation. The Baptism at Jordan stands for the second Initiation. The Transfiguration on the Mount is the symbol for the third, and the Crucifixion represents the fourth. The fifth Initiation, the Resurrection, is the name given to the Initiation which makes a man a Master and the Ascension is the Initiation which takes the Resurrected Master into a still higher stage. The Christ has lived for thousands of years in a Resurrected body and has been an Ascended Master for 2,000 years.

The Crucifixion on the Cross was the outer manifestation of the inner experience of the Great Renunciation or Crucifixion Initiation of the Disciple Jesus. At the same time it was also the outer manifestation of the Ascension Initiation of the Christ. After the Resurrection He appeared once again to the disciples in Galilee. Thomas was asked to put his hand in His side and see that He was solid and physical. He could appear and disappear at will. All of that was an illustration of the Resurrected body, a body of Light.

The interesting thing about the shroud, from my point of view, is how the image was made. The Christ resurrected the body of the Disciple Jesus. When the body was laid in the tomb, the Christ, Maitreya, entered on the third morning. His consciousness once again entered into the body of the Disciple Jesus and brought it back to life—as He had done before with Lazarus—only that wasn't Resurrection. Lazarus was simply brought back to life. This happens—I don't say frequently—but it has happened quite often since, and before. But Resurrection is a very special thing technically. It is a great occult happening.

What the Christ did was not only to bring the body to life again, but also to Resurrect it. He shook loose, if you like, by the down-flow of tremendous spiritual energy into the now dead body of Jesus, the atomic particles of matter, reconstituted these, and brought into that body matter of sub-atomic vibrational rate, that is matter which is literally light. The effect of that on the body was one of intense radiation and it was that radiation which produced what is called an ionisation effect of the image on the shroud.

There is a process in photography called ionisation. When a photographer wants to transfer a negative image to a positive image, or vice versa, he takes the plate and puts it under very high frequency—usually X-rays. The effect of this very high frequency ray bombardment is to ionise the plate so that when it is developed you get the opposite of what you would expect to find. Whatever should be light becomes dark, and whatever should be dark becomes light. The high spiritual down-flow from the Christ into the body of the Disciple Jesus caused the ionisation effect and produced the negative on the shroud—and in this way it is, as it were, scorched on to the shroud, but only on the surface. It is exact, in a way that no photograph could be, and it appeared whether the shroud touched the body or not. It was an ionisation of all aspects of the body, with the wounds and the blood and everything else. So you get an exact facsimile which the space scientists in America have been able to reproduce as a three-dimensional image on the computer. It obeys exactly the three-dimensional laws, and its coming to light now in this exact scientific manner is one of the signs that the Christ is in the world, although His coming into the world is not dependent on that sign.

5/7/77

Have you anything to say about the Holy Father in Rome?

The Master Jesus will take over the throne of St. Peter in Rome, and the true apostolic succession will begin. This event is now imminent, following the Declaration of the Christ. It could well be that the present Pope will be the last.

Note, January 1979: The decease of Pope Paul VI, and the sudden death of Pope John Paul after one month as Pontiff, makes it more than likely that the present Pope, John Paul II, will be the last.

WHAT CAN WE DO *NOW?*

15/7/76

What am I supposed to do now that I know the Christ is to be amongst us? Do I wait for Him to make things perfect or is there something I can be getting on with?

The Masters will not make everything perfect. The Christ will not make everything perfect. You can do what everyone can do—that is, use your spiritual intuition in such a way that you find the best means of service—according to your talents, your point of evolution, your likes, your personality, your temperament, and so on. Find for yourself a field of service, which will be put at the service of the Christ or the Hierarchy, and work that way. It might be the transmission of the energies; or by way of bearing witness, if you like—affirming the *fact* of the Christ. Those who believe in what I am talking about should from now on affirm the *fact* of the Christ, of the World Teacher; affirm the *fact* of Hierarchy, and the *fact* of the imminent reappearance in the world of the Christ and the Hierarchy. If we believe it, this is what we should do, because there is a very tight time schedule involved in this preparation work. The time between now and the reappearance of the Christ is very short indeed. Recently, this has been brought forward until the Christ is virtually in the world—so near is His reappearance. The first five Masters are coming into the world this year. Of course, They won't declare Themselves, but Their work will start in the five Centres this year.

What can you do? You can learn the Great Invocation, if you don't already use it. This invokes tremendous energies into the world. You can join groups—work with groups who meditate; tune into the energies; work in the way of service along some line—humanitarian, or political, or economic, or whatever. It depends on your own background and experience. If you have the desire to serve you will find a way of serving. This is inevitable. It is difficult for me to tell you exactly what to do because I don't know you, I don't know the line of least resistance for you; but if you desire to serve, you will be used. Where there is a genuine, altruistic, aspiring desire to serve humanity, make no mistake about it, this will be known to the Hierarchy and They will use you. They are looking for, and using, all the *practical* mystics in the world. The emphasis is on the word practical. Practical mystics, of whatever tradition and background, are needed. The Masters work with Their disciples in every field: the political, economic, religious, educational, scientific; the occult, the social, the cultural fields. In all these areas the Masters have Their disciples, and They work through them. They look for the aspiring man of goodwill to serve the Plan.

Goodwill is a dynamic energy. The energy we call goodwill is one of the most potent factors in changing world conditions. It is the highest aspect of the energy we call love which mankind is, generally, able to express. When it is made dynamic by the first aspect, the Will aspect, the Will-to-Good, it becomes a tremendous dynamic energy, and it is now changing the world. It is the goodwill of ordinary men and women everywhere which will change the world. They will lead their leaders into the new age. See yourself as a dynamic unit of goodwill in the world. Work with others. Join groups and work with others along these lines. *The new world has to be made by man himself.* Take part in the work of transforming the world.

4/4/78

You say if we feel we believe what you say we should do something about it. Can you give any point to this other than at the moment trying to live in the right way?

This is difficult because everyone has to do it in their own way and from their own level of belief. If you are absolutely certain that the Christ is in the world, as I am, then you will know what to do—you really will know what to do—and you will move heaven and earth to do it. If you think it is a very likely

98

possibility but you are not totally, utterly convinced, then make it known on that level. If you think it is a possibility that the Christ is in the world, do it on that level. At whatever level you can accept it, so you will be proportionately inspired to work. If you really believe it, then tell everyone you meet, everyone who will listen, that you believe that the Christ is in the world—that Maitreya is in the world. It depends whom you are talking to: if you are talking to Jews you will call Him the Messiah. If you are talking to Christians you will call Him the Christ. To Hindus you will call Him the Bodhisattva; to Buddhists, the Lord Maitreya; to Moslems, the Imam Mahdi.

Put it into the garb, the clothes, that the person can understand, and make it as simple as possible. Just state that you believe it. Obviously, you can't prove it. But if you believe it, pass that on. The more people who believe it and pass that belief on, the more people will be inspired by the hope that that engenders. Because this lifts the *hope* of mankind.

Today mankind is so fearful, so desperate. Until recently, there was no hope. I think until President Sadat went to Jerusalem, there was no hope in the world. But since that initiative, which was directly inspired by the Christ, and was His first major political move after July (1977) when He came in, the world has changed. There is a different atmosphere in the world. In Rhodesia, extraordinary things are taking place. This was not to be for twenty years. It was not to be in the lifetime of Mr. Smith. Now he is sitting down in a black government. *Détente* is taking place in the world between East and West—conscious and deliberate *détente*. Obviously, they are still going to show the point of a gun to each other—to keep each other informed that it is there, and that they are strong, but fundamentally, they have accepted *détente*. This is new, entirely new. There is a new, growing hope in the world, but to know that the Christ is in the world will lift and uphold the hope of mankind as nothing else can.

There is nothing better you can do than to say, "I believe it". Shout it from the housetops! Write to the newspapers and say you believe this; write to whomever you like and say you believe it. To spread His Messages and make them known throughout the world is the best way to do this. That is why they are given—to proclaim the fact that He has returned and to outline His Teachings. Send these to friends and contacts everywhere and ask them to do the same. In this way is built the atmosphere of hope and expectancy in which the Christ can most quickly emerge and teach.

4/4/78

Don't you need to be careful not to be labelled a crack-pot or you will destroy the message?

Very soon the crack-pots will become heroes. I have been speaking publicly for the past three years and I have done my best not to seem a crack-pot. I have tried to be reasonable, rational, and I think I still am reasonable and rational, but inevitably, some people will construe what I am saying as being demented. But these are the people who are going to say when they see the Christ, "That's not the Christ. Where is His long robe. Where are the holes in His hands?" But where people are open, then say:"I believe it. I believe it." Affirm His Presence! Send the "Messages of the Christ" to all your friends and acquaintances. Make these preliminary Teachings known, and prepare the Way for Him.

THE ANTI-CHRIST. THE FORCES OF EVIL

26/4/77

There is a great deal of talk about the Anti-Christ. Can you say something about this?

There is such a thing as the Anti-Christ, but there is a great misapprehension about what the Anti-Christ is. Fundamentally, the Anti-Christ is the First or Will aspect of God, in its destructive form. It is that which destroys in order to prepare the way for the building aspect, which is the Christ aspect. It is that which breaks down and destroys the old to prepare the new forms for the incoming energy, the building energy, so that the Christ aspect can manifest. That is what is happening now. This Anti-Christ force has worked out through the war from 1914–1945. (From the Hierarchical point of view that was one war.) That war was precipitated on to the physical plane from the astral planes where it had been going on, since Atlantean times, between the Forces of Light and the Forces of Darkness; the evolutionary and the involutionary forces; the Hierarchy and the materialistic forces of this planet. The war between them in Atlantis caused the Hierarchy (Who before then had worked openly, outwardly in the world as the priest-kings and god-like beings Who gave men the Atlantean civilisation), to become occult, esoteric, working only from the higher mental planes. By the defeat of the Axis powers in the war of 1939–1945, the Forces of Evil of the planet (which is the evil of *all* mankind, not simply of the Axis powers), were defeated. Certain leaders in Nazi Germany, Japan, and to a much lesser extent in Italy, focused in themselves the energy which we call the Anti-Christ; but it is an energy, it is not a being, not an individual. It is preparing the way. It is the destructive force of God Himself, which prepares the way for the Christ.

Where the involutionary force overflows on to the evolu-

101

tionary arc (on which we are), it appears to us as evil. It has its role, in upholding the matter aspect of the planet, but too gross a materiality prevents mankind from advancing along the evolutionary path.

The Forces of Evil on the planet have been defeated. They are not destroyed, but they are defeated. There is a stanza in the Great Invocation which says: "And may it seal the door where evil dwells". This refers to the sealing energies (which we transmitted earlier in the meeting). Their job is to lock away, to seal those forces to their own domain, to uphold the matter aspect, by lifting humanity above the level where they can be influenced, so that we can spiritualise matter, which is what we are really about.

27/1/76

Are you saying evil will cease to exist?

No, I am not saying that evil will cease to exist, not yet anyway. The forces of evil on the planet have been defeated. The defeat of the Axis powers in the great war from 1939 to 1945 represented the defeat on the physical plane of the forces of evil. They are not totally destroyed, but they are defeated. Since 1966 the energetic strength of the forces of Light has been greater than that of the forces of darkness. The forces of darkness have always had an advantage over the Hierarchy, who represent the forces of Light, because they work on the physical plane. Whereas the Hierarchy, since Atlantean times, when They became occult, work on the consciousness planes, on the higher mental planes. So Their hands have been somewhat tied in relation to man's life on the physical plane. But since 1966 a balance has been achieved and the forces of Light are now stronger in the world.

The Masters can now come out into the world and work with humanity on the physical plane, and add Their power to the existing power of the disciples and men of goodwill.

The forces of evil can now be sealed off to their own domain, the upholding of the matter aspect of the planet. The true Armageddon, the final battle between these two forces, will be fought out on mental levels in the middle of the Capricornian Age.

5/3/76

Are the forces of evil just a part of God?

Of course, yes, the forces of evil are part of God. They are not separate from God. Everything is God. There is nothing else in fact but God. The forces of evil on this planet receive their energy from the cosmic astral plane. They are fundamentally the forces of materiality, the forces of matter. They are part of the involutionary process of Deity, involving Itself in matter and producing the pairs of opposites—Spirit on the one hand, and Matter on the other.

5/3/76

Why are the forces of darkness trying to stop the initiation of mankind? Are you inferring that the forces of darkness are man's animal ego?

No. The forces of darkness, the forces of evil—what we call evil, the involutionary force of the planet—has its place—in upholding the matter aspect of the planet. But an overflow of that—a gross materiality, is inimical to the spiritual progress of the race. Mankind is on the evolutionary arc. It is moving out of matter, and too great an overflow of this evil on to the evolutionary arc could destroy this planet. In fact, without the help of certain great energies, great Entities, who have been called into the world by the Lord of Shamballa Himself, this planet would have perished before now, due to the action of the forces of evil whose purpose is to destroy. They work against the evolutionary plan because it seals their fate.

Oh, so you are giving them a separate animation?

Indeed. They are very highly conscious entities. They are as conscious and as active in their line as the Masters of the Wisdom are in Theirs.

And yet not separate from God?

103

And yet not separate from God. Of course not. But God involved in matter. The involutionary force, God in Its involutionary aspect.

26/4/77

What is the place of Satan, and the Final Judgement?

Well, I can only speak from my own perspective. Satan and the Judgement rests with every man; each one is his own Satan, each his own judge. Every action, every thought, sets in motion causes, the effects of which make your life for good or ill. This is the great Law of Cause and Effect, which the Christ will demonstrate once again. He said before—"as you sow, so shall you reap". Once again He will demonstrate that this law is totally bound up with the whole of our existence.

Are you referring to reincarnation perhaps?

Yes. This is the Law of Rebirth, which we call reincarnation. It is through the Law of Cause and Effect that we come again and again into incarnation as souls, demonstrating on the physical plane through the personality. The fact that we create on this plane certain effects, set in motion certain causes, ties us to this plane and draws us repeatedly till these are resolved. In this way the whole of our evolutionary life is acted out, until gradually, through the experience of this evolutionary path, we perfect ourselves, revealing more and more of our divine nature.

Each time we die we see our high self, our true Self. We come face to face with our soul; we see our life as it has been; we see the purposes which the soul had for coming into incarnation. We always come into incarnation with three major purposes, which it is the aim of the soul that we manifest. We see these, and we can measure how much of any of these purposes we have in fact fulfilled. This is really the true judgement. This happens life after life until we perfect ourselves, and need no longer incarnate on this planet. Then we are Masters.

The Final Judgement will come at the end of the Earth's seventh and last cycle or round, when all but a remnant of Humanity will have Achieved, become perfected Masters.

104

HOW DO YOU KNOW THIS?

7/3/78

If it is important to get this word around why isn't this information given to more prominent people—with all due respect to you?

There is a good reason why someone who is really quite unknown in the world is given this information. It is very important that humanity's free will is not infringed. If this information had been given to President Carter, or the Duke of Edinburgh, or the Queen, or someone very, very, well-known, with a tremendous following, and they said the Christ is in the world, millions would believe it because they said it—because Jimmy Carter said it, or the Duke of Edinburgh said it. That could be construed as infringing human free will. If I say it, I have no authority except the authority of my conviction. My contact with Hierarchy is my own personal authority, but that is nothing to you, do you see? It is only an unknown person speaking to groups and to the public, making certain statements about the reappearance of the Christ. You can take it or leave it. You hear it, you think about it, and if it seems right to you you accept it; and if it doesn't seem right you reject it. There has been no infringement of your free will. You are at total liberty to accept it or reject it. But if somebody really well-known, like the Duke of Edinburgh, or President Carter, or the Pope, said the Christ was in the world—well, if the Pope said it, then every Catholic in the world would believe him and there would be a weight of authority which would infringe their free will. Likewise if President Carter said it.

It has to be your own intuitive response to what one is saying. You have to know and you have to recognise the Christ for what He is. Not because President Carter, or the Pope, or whoever, said He is in the world, but because you have in you the qualities that that man says the world needs. He will be saying we have to share, we have to co-operate; mankind has to be free; we have to have justice in the world; we must feed the starving millions; our brothers are dying in their millions and we do nothing. This is what the Christ will say. And you have to say, that man is my man—whether you recognise that He is the Christ or not. Because the Christ Consciousness is working through you. You must *want* what He is advocating. It has to be that way. It has to be mankind's own response, from man's own free will.

17/2/77

You're not the reincarnation of John the Baptist, by any chance?

I am not the reincarnation of John the Baptist.

How do you know you are not?

I know, believe me. John the Baptist is long since a Master, and in fact is no longer on the Earth.

30/8/77

Where have you got your information from?

A Senior Member of the Hierarchy. One of that Group Who surround the Christ.

4/10/77

The technique that you've just talked about—your receiving the communication from the Christ—sounds very much like you have an electrical antenna at the top of your head and that, tuning in at one level you're communicating with your Master, but higher up you're tuning in with the Christ. Now, are you in perfect communication with your Master all the time, virtually?

Yes, all the time. He has trained me and prepared me in a certain way for this work, which entails a moment to moment contact with Him, and, over the past few years, this kind of communication from the Christ, preparatory to these public transmissions of His Messages.

Do any of the members of the Hierarchy or the Masters ever speak to man through mediums in trance?

Very, very rarely. It is one of the ways with which They prefer not to work. There are a few cases, indeed, where They have done so. One of the most famous and wonderful is the use of a man called "The Boy". Those who have read the book by Swami Omananda, *The Boy and the Brothers*, will know whom I mean. He was a slum child from the East End of London, a great Initiate, in fact of the fourth degree, and in his incarnation before Liberation. He suffered a great deal. He was an empty shell, simply a hollow personality, which was taken over by the Masters.

They do not normally use this method. They use telepathy which is the higher clairvoyance, through the medium of the soul. It was in this way that H. P. Blavatsky was given "The Secret Doctrine" by the Master D. K.; in this way Alice Bailey was given the Teachings by D. K.; it was in this way, too, that Helena Roerich was given the Agni Yoga Teachings. This is the normal mode. There are occasionally individuals who use the higher kind of trance. In very special cases. The usual lower psychism is never used by the Masters. It is used by entities on the inner planes, of course, on some level of the astral or mental planes, but not by the Masters Themselves. It is only on the higher mental planes that the Masters can be contacted. They work only from the higher mental, not from the astral level.

Has this group a special role to play as individuals?

This group is formed to do a special function which is to help prepare the way for the Christ. To prepare the way in this country and through this country, so far as we are able, the rest of the world. It is formed specifically for that purpose. It has other purposes, but that is its immediate role.

We act, too, as a bridge between Hierarchy and the world—transmitting the energy from Hierarchy and giving the information from Hierarchy. The last information about the return of the Christ was given up to 1949 by Alice A. Bailey—through the Alice Bailey Teachings. That was given to her by the Master D. K.

Now the working out of the Plan today, and the fact of the Christ's Presence in the world has been given to me by my own Master, and of course, since September 6th 1977, publicly, by Maitreya Himself, through His Messages.

28/3/78

I wondered, when you are overshadowed by the Christ, is He perhaps sitting in the place where He is in the modern world, sending out the message now, to you?

He is where He is, in a well-known country, and part of His consciousness—I can't tell you how much—probably a tiny, miniscule part of His mental and emotional make-up—because it is not only mental, but also an astral overshadowing—comes as a light, descends as a light. Some of you may have seen it, if you are clairvoyant. It descends on me and comes down as far as the solar plexus and a kind of cone is formed, like that, in light. There is an emotional outflow as well. It is the mental overshadowing which produces the rapport so that I can hear, inwardly, the words. The astral overshadowing allows what is called the True Spirit of the Christ, the energy of the Cosmic Christ, to flow out to the audience and through the audience to the world. So there are two things taking place. Of course He remains where He is. Part of His consciousness is here and when He says "I am with you once more" He means it literally. I am aware of His Presence, I can sense part of His mind in my mind. It is difficult to describe, but it is there.

22/3/78

Can you give us some idea of how many centres there are in the world, where talks and messages are being given out, like this?

At this moment, not one. This is the only one where the Christ is giving messages like this *in public*. It is my understanding that in each of the Five Centres (London, New York, Tokyo, Darjeeling and Geneva) there is someone like me giving information about the return of the Christ—in different ways. Not necessarily as I have given it tonight, not necessarily esoterically. It could be given wrapped up in a more traditional, more orthodox teaching. And, so far, not publicly. I am told that one Centre is only half functioning, so there are really four and a half of us.

22/3/78

Are there any reasons why this isn't being carried on in other very large centres like Paris, or New York?

Well, it was supposed to go out through the Five Centres. I understand that the other centres are not so active, not so organised as, happily, we are here. I don't know why that is. It has happened that we are somewhat—I believe, quite a lot—better organised, more vocal, more public about this information than the other centres, where it tends to be by word of mouth, privately, not by public meetings like this.

Nevertheless, this information is getting to people all over the world now. Since July last year people have written and telephoned me to say, "I believe what you say, because in my meditation I have received some kind of vision". There is some kind of inner conviction or prompting which makes them believe that, in fact, the Christ is now in the world. I also know that this information which I have been giving out has become very strongly focused as a thought-form on the various astral and mental planes, so that now you will find it coming through many of the mediums in the world.

GOD

There is no reason to believe that man is alone in the universe.

There is, on the contrary, every reason to believe that there exists, behind all outer appearances, an immense Consciousness to which we give the name of God. The testimony of all the Sages and Teachers, down the ages, points to this being so.

Any other conclusion would leave out the experience of the most gifted and aware men produced by the race, which would be a foolish thing to do if one values men of the highest calibre.

28/3/78

You use the word God quite frequently. Could you give your view of what you mean by God? Can you define God?

Curiously enough we don't often get this question but we got it last week, and then I said that this was probably the most difficult question to answer—who am I to say what God is? If I can say anything about It at all, I would say that in a sense there is no such thing as God, God does not exist. And in another sense, there is nothing else but God—only God exists.

God to me—I am speaking intellectually now, from which angle one cannot know God, but since you have asked me for a definition (you have asked for the impossible, but I shall attempt it)—God is the sum total of all the laws, and all the energies governed by these laws, which make up the whole of the manifested and unmanifested universe—everything we know and see and hear and touch and everything we don't know or hear or see or touch, everywhere, in the totality of cosmos. Every manifested phenomenon is part of God. And the space between these manifested phenomena is God. So, in a very real sense, there isn't anything else. You are God. I am God. This microphone is God. This table is God. All is God. And because all is God, there is no God. God is not someone that you can

110

point to and say "That is God". God is everything that you have ever known or could ever know—and everything beyond your level of knowing.

That God, unmanifested, uncreated, desires to know Itself in all Its possibilities, Its possible aspects, and takes incarnation—gradually involves Itself in that opposite pole of Itself which we call matter. Spirit and matter are two poles of Reality or God. Both are part of the same totality. But as they go further and further in polarity—distance from themselves—we get the pairs of opposites. We get good and evil, we get night and day, we get spirit and matter, and so on. We are locked in the dilemma of the pairs of opposites. Through the meditational process—which takes us eventually into the knowledge of, and at-one-ment with, the soul aspect of ourselves, the divine aspect—we can resolve these two apparent opposites. In that resolution we stand between the two. That is is where the Knower stands—knowing that there is neither good nor evil, knowing that there is only One, there is only God. So you can come to know God in a certain way—but no one can talk about it.

God cannot be known from the level from which I am speaking now. It is impossible. God can, I believe, be sensed and apprehended as an experience, from moment to moment only, as *That which IS when we go beyond our thought and abide in that state of unthinking awareness of the totality, without sense of self*. Then we can know God. Most of us, at the stage where we are, can know It perhaps for a fraction of a second or a few moments, but that second or few moments will give one the sense of Its immortality and Its infinity. That is all one can say about that experience afterwards. You cannot describe it. As soon as you describe it you are describing a memory, you are describing an experience which is no longer God. It is something which cannot be talked about, It can only be known from moment to moment.

Certain individuals, the Christ for example, can show you what God is like. This is what Christ in Palestine and the Buddha showed. They showed what God is like, in certain aspects. Only aspects, even the Christ can only show aspects. He comes now to show a higher aspect than even the Love

111

aspect which He showed before. It is a greater aspect, a more inclusive aspect of God, which He will reveal to mankind. This is the New Revelation.

30/9/76

But really, everything comes from within. This idea that God is sort of "out there" is absolutely false really, isn't it?

We shall see that God is within, as you say—within us and around us and also within and around everyone and everything else. At the same time we shall realise God as a Transcendent *Principle*, the Source of all Being, manifest in the phenomenal world and yet uncreated, unmanifest, behind all.

We shall also come to understand God in the planetary sense—as Sanat Kumara, the Lord of the world on Shamballa, the Reflection of our Planetary Logos or Deity; and come before Him at the third Initiation.

8/3/77

If God were omnipresent, this would be Heaven. Why is there suffering?

You are a soul incarnating on the physical plane, through a personality, with a physical, an emotional, and a mental vehicle. All of these make up your personality, the reflection on this plane of a great god, your own soul—which is identical with the Logos of this planet of which we are all part. The reason we suffer, fundamentally, is because we think we are separate. Because we believe and experience ourselves as separate from God. If we could, from moment to moment, as the Masters of the Wisdom do, as the highest Initiates do, experience ourselves as one with all that exists, One, and identical, we would realise that we and God are One. We would no longer suffer.

If God is immanent in all of creation, He is physically in us. What is physical is a part of God at a certain level. What we call the physical world is God, manifesting at a certain level, at this level of consciousness. God at the soul level of consciousness is manifesting in a much more perfect way and if we had perfect

112

soul consciousness, if we had perfect God consciousness, we would realise that we and God are One. There is no separation. But because we identify with the personality, and with this body with its suffering and its hopes and fears and its ambitions and so on, because we identify with that, we suffer; because that is the level that we reduce God to, through identification. It *is* a part of God—because there isn't anything outside God.

But the part cannot see the Whole in its entirety. If we can bring that part—that physical plane personality—into soul-infusion, we become Initiate, we become aware of God and manifest that God in Its true state.

This is the perfectioning process of evolution, in which we are all engaged, the process which the Masters of the Wisdom have finished. They have arrived at that point; They are totally at-one with God. They know God from moment to moment because That is what They identify with. They do not suffer. What I am suggesting to you tonight, is that They are an example for us, so that we, too, shall come to the same point. We are only suffering now because we are identifying with the lower aspect of ourselves, rather than with the higher aspect. But this is an evolutionary process. We can't do it all at once. This is why reincarnation, the Doctrine of Rebirth, is a fact; why from life to life we need to undergo experience, to gradually become soul-infused and perfected.

27/1/76

Will the final goal of complete identification with the Godhead ever be achieved, or will these cycles continue eternally?

It is achieved individually. Eventually, every man will achieve this identity with Godhead. You are really saying: "what is the final Plan?" Well, the final Plan is in the Mind of the Logos Himself, and up to now we can only sense a tiny little part of it, that part which is revealed through the Indicators of the Plan, who are the Buddha and the Christ, the great Masters Who have shown us what the Plan is, what the Will of God is for us. I would say that ultimately, this planet has to perfect Itself; that we have evil on this planet because the planet Itself is not

113

totally, in every aspect of Its Being, perfect; totally at-one with the Solar Logos—which Itself is not perfect.

There is a hierarchy throughout the whole of cosmos. Compared with Sirius, for instance, our solar system is a novice, a very unevolved system. Compared with a planet like Venus, this planet is very unevolved. In the same way compared with the Masters, we are very unevolved, but compared with early, animal man, we are really quite advanced. Millions on this planet now are standing on the threshold of a great step into the spiritual kingdom. That means an enormous expansion of consciousness for humanity as a whole.

27/1/76

So then do you say that the evolution of man can be involved in aiding the evolution of this planet?

Oh, inevitably. It has to be. Yes. That's its function.

Goal of our Evolution

27/1/76

What will be the eventual goal of this planet, in its evolution?

One day we shall know God. We shall know God really, when we have lifted ourselves, occultly, through the process of Initiation, through the agency of the Christ and the Masters. This planet will shine like a jewel in the heavens, and from it will radiate a particular kind of energy, a specific ray in its purity. This planet, like all planets, is governed by a particular ray, and absorbs and radiates energies. But necessarily, at the moment, since it is not perfect, since it is not even a sacred planet, the light emitted from this planet is dulled. The ray potency is relatively low. The quality of the colour is fragmentary, impure. One day, through the agency of man, this planet will shine with the brilliance of a diamond. That is the ultimate aim of this planet—to shine in the heavens in its absolutely pure form, radiating its specific ray in total purity.

To what extent does God choose to act or speak to man directly and to what extent does He act through intermediaries like the Hierarchy you describe?

God always works through agents. Always. This is true for every manifestation of God. As soon as God comes into incarnation, manifests Itself at whatever level, it works through some agency or other. Itself it is unmanifest and yet is immanent in everything that is manifest. The Christ is an agent. The Christ is not God. When I say, "the coming of Christ", I don't mean the coming of God, I mean the coming of a divine man, a man who has manifested His divinity by the same process that we are going through—the incarnational process, gradually perfecting Himself; the Initiatory process, gradually becoming more and more divine. Initiation allows a man entry, bit by bit, into the Mind of God. He becomes more and more aware of the nature of Reality and so more and more divine—exhibits more and more of that divinity. The Masters have done this to the point where They are what we call perfect, but it is a relative perfection. To us they are perfect because They have finished the experiences of this planet. But They see great realms above Them, states of Being of which we can know nothing. The Christ is the Master of all the Masters, but He is not God, and never claimed to be God. He is a Son of God, but then so are we. But He knows He is, and manifests it.

To me, God is the sum total of all that exists in the whole of the manifested and unmanifested universe. That unmanifest, when in incarnation, manifest, is the Christos, the Christ Principle, the great Evolutionary Principle. That energy—because it is an energy (there isn't anything else)—is not a man, but manifests through men. Maitreya, the Christ, is the Embodiment of That Principle on this planet.

God can only work through agents. The degree of Divinity manifested is entirely dependent on the status of the agent, the closeness of the agent to the Divine Mind through at-one-ment. This is the origin of hierarchy.

What do you mean by God?

There are three suns—the outer physical sun that we see; the inner heart of the sun from which flows that energy which we call Love. The Christ Principle, the Christ Consciousness, flows from the heart of the sun. That is the Son aspect of God. Then there is a Central Spiritual Sun, God the Father, in Christian terms, from which flows the Highest Spiritual Will. These three together make the Being of the Logos of our solar system. That is God in systemic terms. When I talked about God I brought It a bit nearer, and talked about God in planetary terms, because this planet is actually a vehicle of expression for a Cosmic Entity, a great Heavenly Man. It is a Centre in the body of God of our solar system, just as our heart centre is a centre in our system. The planetary Logos is a little God in a bigger God which is the systemic Logos—which Itself is only a little God in an even greater galactic system—at the centre of which is another greater God. There is a Hierarchy. That is where Hierarchy comes from. There is a gradation of divinity from the lowest crystal of the mineral world up to and beyond the Galactic God Himself, about Whom we can say nothing at all. That is not a man but a Great Consciousness.

30/8/77

Could you say something about the Logos of this planet and the Logos of the Solar system?

The Logos of this planet is a great heavenly Being—a Heavenly Man. Eighteen and a half million years ago, He took physical incarnation on this planet, on the etheric physical planes (etheric matter is still physical). On the two highest of these planes is a great centre of energy which is called Shamballa, the Centre where the Will of God is known. The Logos is reflected as a Being on Shamballa, as the Lord of the World, the Ancient of Days, of the Bible. He has many names—Sanat Kumara; the Lord of the World; the Youth of Endless Summers; the King;

116

the One Initiator; the Great Sacrifice. He has sacrificed Himself—He comes from Venus—for 18½ million years so far, to enable the Plan of the Logos to work out on this planet in an altogether more potent way.

Sanat Kumara is both the Logos and not the Logos. He is the energetic equivalent, the reflection, of the Logos but He is not the personality of the Logos. The Logos has no personality aspect. The Masters, too, don't have a personality in our meaning of the word. They are living souls. They give expression only to the soul and Monadic nature. Likewise with Sanat Kumara, only on an altogether higher level. He is the reflection on the physical plane of the Logos, so to all intents and purposes He *is* the Logos. But the Logos Himself, is a Cosmic Being who ensouls this planet, Whose body of expression it is. Everything in it on every level, from the densest physical to the highest spiritual level—all of that—is the expression of the thought in the mind of a great Cosmic Being. That is our immediate Planetary Logos.

He Himself is a centre in the body of expression of an even greater Cosmic Being Who is the Solar Logos—Who in His turn stands in relation to the Logos of Sirius as our personality stands in relation to our soul. Our personality is a reflection of the soul on its level. In the same way, only on a cosmic level, this solar system is the reflection of an even greater Being Who ensouls Sirius. Just as our soul on its level is a reflection of an even greater Being which we call the Monad or Spirit, the spark of God, so Sirius itself is a reflection. We are really threefold—spirit, soul, and personality. Likewise with the solar systems: there is a triangle formed in the heavens between this solar system—as the lowest expression, at the densest level—and Sirius, at what corresponds to the soul level in man, and the Great Bear, which corresponds to the Monad or Spirit in man. That is a great cosmic triangle, and the energies of the Seven Rays are actually the expression of the Lives of seven great Beings Who ensoul seven stars in the Great Bear. That kind of formation is repeated throughout cosmos.

The Logos of this System is on the Second Ray of Love-Wisdom, so that for this Solar System, God is Love. All

117

other Rays are expressing Themselves as sub-rays of this basic Love Ray which synthesises them all.

The great Law of Cause and Effect comes from Sirius, is generated by the Cosmic energy of Sirius, of which our solar system is the reflection.

Grace

22/9/77

What is the occult or esoteric equivalent or definition of what the churches call Grace?

In the Eastern tradition, of course, there is also Grace. There is the Grace of the Guru—when the Guru bestows his blessing, you have Grace. Grace is really the transmission of energy. When a guru—a Master or a guru, whatever you call him—bestows his blessing on his disciples he transmits energy to them. They live in the glow of his love, and that is an energy—not simply in his affection, as it were, but in the actual glow and response to the energy of his love. That is Grace.

It is precisely the same kind of Grace which Christians think of as being in a state of grace. It is being in a state in which you are pure in heart and in mind and therefore can receive the love of the guru, in this case the Christ; the Christ is the guru of Christians. He is also the guru, as Maitreya, of the Buddhists. It is that transmission of energy, that unbroken line of contact from heart to heart that conveys Grace.

When a man is not in a state of Grace, he feels that he has sinned; and unfortunately, an awful lot of people think they are not in a state of Grace because they have been conditioned into experiencing sins which are not really sins, would not be sins to most people, but they cloud the heart; it is only when the heart is unclouded, when the heart is pure, when it is filled with neither guilt nor hate, that you can be in a state of Grace. When you love yourself, but through loving yourself love everything and everyone else, then you are in a state of Grace; then the heart is pure, the pure rays of Love from the higher sources (the agencies of which are the gurus—the Christ, the Buddha, and many other gurus of lesser degree), streaming ultimately from Deity Itself, flow in. Then the connection is made, and you stand in a state of grace.

I think that statement of yours "clouding the heart" is a very penetrating and apt way of putting it. Some people say they walk in a shadow, and then they have an experience of somebody who really has got, even on a low level, love for them and that shadow goes away.

Yes, it lifts the guilt, the self-hate, and through the self-hate the hate of others—the hate of others is simply the projection of the self-hate.

Some people have difficulty forgiving themselves. What can they do about it?

Start forgiving themselves. Men must realise, and will realise under the tutorship of the Masters and the Christ, that Divinity is a gradation. Men don't forgive themselves because they have had instilled in them from childhood, the idea of perfection in behaviour—at every stage from birth upwards; and that they have somehow to be, if they are Christians, like Christ; or if they are Buddhists, like Buddha, and so on—which of course is impossible. We cannot be like Christ all at once, but we can be like Christ in potential; and one of the problems is that the churches have removed Christ from humanity. The orthodox teaching down the ages is that the Christ is now sitting "up there" somewhere in Heaven, on the right hand of God, and you can know Him only by the reports of His work in Palestine: how He died for our sins, and so: "Little sinner, if you sin you're denying that terrible sacrifice that He made", and so on. It is a tremendous pressure of guilt which is inflicted on people, so they can't forgive themselves for stealing two prunes. From infancy this great weight of guilt is put on us. Whereas, the Christ should have been presented by the churches as He is—as a living, acting, working, present man in the world; a divine man, but divine in exactly the sense that we are divine; only we

119

have it in potential while He has manifested it, perfected Himself and *achieved* that divinity. That is the difference between Him and us. But in doing it He is the guarantee that we shall also do it, that it is possible.

So it is easier to be divine and it is easier to be Christ-like than the churches believe, and at the same time it is more difficult. Just to say "Be like Christ" or "Be good", or whatever, doesn't make it possible; they haven't shown the way. They say: "Do what I tell you", but that is not showing the way. The Christ will show the way—what was it He said last week? He will show that "the way to God is a simple path which all men can tread". It is like that, a simple path which all men can take—religious and non-religious men—those whose way is through politics or economics or education, and so on, not necessarily through religion at all. The path to God is broad enough to take in all men.

In my experience, and as some of you will know, I have been talking about the imminence of the Reappearance of the Christ for the last three years, I have found that people desperately want the Christ to be in the world, but they are afraid at the very thought. It fills them with awe, and it fills them with fear; so that many reject what they most deeply want, because they feel: "I could not stand before the Christ as I know I truly am, and face that One"—forgetting that as the Lord of Love He is also the Lord of Forgiveness; not only that, but He doesn't even judge. He knows it all, and where has He been all this time anyway. They've not been hidden from Him. It's not as if He is seeing them for the first time.

But the church would say that's a blasphemy, wouldn't they?

Indeed; well, if it's blasphemy, it's blasphemy. So much for blasphemy! Soon all men will know that the Christ is a very simple man, and is not a judge. He comes because He loves humanity. That is the basic reason for His Return—because it is the Will of God, and because He loves humanity. He is responding to the cry for help from humanity, which rose to Him during and after the war and is still rising, and He has answered that call. But He comes as a very simple man, who,

120

because He is Who He is, can see through all our little difficulties, and loves us nevertheless—just as a mother knows all the little stealings and lie-telling that the children do, but she loves the child nevertheless, if she has any sense. It's like that, it really is like that.

THE LAW OF LOVE

12/10/79

Could you say more about the Law of Love and its implementation?

The Law of Love, according to the Hierarchy, is the basic law governing our existence. We live in a solar system Whose nature is Love. The Christ came 2,000 years ago to show a new aspect of God, that aspect we call Love. He showed God as a loving father—not an old man with a beard, of course—Whose nature is essentially Love. Love is an energy, a great cosmic energy which streams from the Heart of the Sun.

There are three suns: the physical sun which we see; the inner Heart of the sun from which flows Love, and the Central Spiritual Sun from which flows Spiritual Will. These three aspects—the Intelligent Activity aspect of the outer sun, the Love aspect of the inner and the Spiritual Will of the Central Spiritual Sun—make up God as we know It in this solar system. Will, Love and Intelligence are God in manifestation.

Each individual, each planet, and each solar system is governed by certain great cosmic streams of force which we call Rays. There are seven. Our soul, personality, our bodies—physical, emotional, and mental—are on one or other of these rays. They can all be different. The Deity ensouling our solar system has as His nature that quality we call Love. It is the very expression of His Being. It is a Second Ray system, the Ray of Love/Wisdom. Its total expression, through all its ramifications, is an expression of Love, synthesising all aspects. Even the Will aspect is a sub-ray of the Second Ray in this solar system.

Love is really a great magnetic, cohesive force. It is the energy which holds the particles of the atoms together. It is that magnetic force which, throughout the universe, attracts to each other these particles—the building blocks of nature. All is

122

sustained and held together *in relationship* by the energy of Love. It is that energy which holds the atoms of our bodies together and makes them cohere in a lawful way, according to the Plan of our Logos, Who has created us. We are thoughts in the mind of the creating Logos of our planet.

That great energy of Love streams all the way from such a cosmic, magnetic force to what we call feeling, amity, affection or love. Love as we understand it is entirely different from the Love the Masters know. They call love "Pure Reason" or Buddhi. It is loving understanding, Love and Wisdom together, a totally impersonal but *all inclusive* cohesive, binding force which draws all men and all things together, and holds them together. It is the energy which makes humanity One. Mankind is not only a unity, it is a unit. It is a fused Being, and each unit in that Being is held together in a dynamic relationship by that energy we call Love. So that it is absolutely intrinsic to our nature. When we demonstrate hatred or anything else but Love we are only demonstrating Love in a distorted fashion. Goodwill is Love on a lower level, hatred is Love on the other side of the coin. That Love is everywhere in the universe; there could not be a universe without the manifestation of the energy we call Love. There are other, higher aspects than Love—and the Christ comes to show a higher aspect which includes Love. That is the New Revelation.

Christ's great work 2,000 years ago was to show man that this Love is his very nature. It is the nature of God, and as he is made in the likeness of God, it is the nature of man. He showed, too, that through the demonstration of that Love, man comes to God, comes to know God, not as an old man sitting up in heaven, but in himself, in his brothers, and all around him. He comes to know that really there is nothing else but God whose nature is Love; and that without it there can be no existence. There could be no world. So that unless we manifest this Love, whose expression is brotherhood, we shall destroy ourselves. This is what the Christ is now saying, and will say. Love is absolutely fundamental to our nature and without its manifestation we cannot continue to live. It is expressed by *right relationship* manifesting through sharing and justice for all.

123

THE SOUL AND REINCARNATION

14/2/78

You mentioned in an earlier meeting that each person comes into incarnation with three main purposes. Can you tell us how one should go about realising these purposes and finding them out?

Through meditation. The way to come into the knowledge of the purpose of any incarnation is to become aware of oneself as a soul, and the way to become aware of oneself as a soul is to meditate. It is through aspiration, through service, and through meditation that the channel between the physical brain and the soul is formed. This is called the antahkarana. Through that channel of light pours the energy of the soul into its vehicle, that is, ourselves, the man or woman in incarnation. With that energy comes the knowledge, the purpose, and the love nature of the soul. As that works out in altruistic service, so the purpose for any given life can become known. I don't mean to say that everyone who meditates is guaranteed that they will know their soul purpose, but that is how it happens when it does happen.

You will find, in practice, that if the soul impulse is strongly manifesting in the personality, the man will be drawn instinctively to some field of service in which his soul purpose, or purposes, can be fulfilled. The soul purpose for all in incarnation at any given time is, of course, the creation of right human relationships.

Service

28/3/78

Why is service so important?

Service is the lever of the evolutionary path. Through service

124

we learn to identify with that which we serve, and so a shift occurs in our centre of focus. It shifts from the personal, the selfish, to the impersonal, the unselfish. And, in doing that, we identify more and more with more and more. The way is through service. That is why it was instituted by the Christ in Palestine, as a lever for the evolutionary process, because, as we begin to serve, we become more and more decentralised, we identify with more and more, until we can identify with everything that is. And when we can identify with everything that is, we *are* everything that is. We are God. We release our Divinity.

19/3/76

It is said that at these change-over points between age and age there are two kinds of souls incarnating, those of the latter age and those of the age—essentially a different batch, so to speak—coming in with the new age and another batch going out.

The majority of souls in incarnation at the moment are Piscean. They are the result of the Piscean experience; but more and more, with every year that passes, souls are coming into incarnation who are essentially Aquarian in outlook, in ray quality. The Piscean age was dominated by the great Sixth Ray of Abstract Idealism or Devotion. This ray is fast moving out but it completely colours all our institutions, all our ideas. It is the strongest ray in influence at the moment; everything is so strongly coloured by it that you can say we are still in the Piscean Age. But every day, the Aquarian energies and the great Seventh Ray of Order or Ritual are coming into manifestation more potently. This brings about synthesis. The Seventh Ray is the ray which relates spirit to matter and synthesises the two. This relating ray is never out of incarnation for very long, never longer than about 1,500 years, and it brings that which is spiritual or idealistic down on to the physical plane and makes it manifest. In the New Age, with this energy tremendously dominant, the ideas and ideals of brotherhood, of sharing, of right relationship, of goodwill, which we have all had as ideals but have not manifested, will be manifested through its agency.

This will be because egos on this ray will, more and more, come into incarnation over the next 2,000 years. (Each age lasts roughly 2,300 years and of course, overlaps; we are in the transitional phase.)

It is a fact that every generation brings into incarnation souls who are equipped with the knowledge, the energy, the "know-how" to deal with the problems they will meet. We are brought into incarnation as groups under law, and groups of relatively highly evolved egos are now being brought into incarnation for the first time for hundreds of years. They are coming now, specifically, to do the work of rehabilitation, of salvaging the world, which is necessary before we can enter into the age of Aquarius in a way fitting to the spiritual nature of that age.

19/3/76

You say groups of souls incarnate into various work of preparation and so on, but presumably there are lots of people in incarnation who perhaps don't have that job of preparation, they haven't reached that level of recognising that there is any kind of work to do at all—are these people also brought into incarnation in groups?

Yes. It is a question, really, of the point of development (as you suggest). The average man is magnetically drawn into incarnation by his desire nature, by that which held him to earth. The strands or ties of karma, the effects of causes which we have set in motion, create groupings, family and wider groupings, which necessitate group incarnation to work out and resolve.

Soul Experience

12/4/77

When a person incarnates do they necessarily use, in any particular life, all the soul experiences which they have accumulated in past lives, or may they be just using part of it?

On soul levels, of course, all that experience is there. There is nothing that has ever happened—no thought, no feeling, no sensation, no experience of any kind—which does not have its reflection, its reverberation, in the causal body, the vehicle of expression of the soul on the causal plane, the highest of the four mental planes. We are, as personalities, vehicles for the soul, just as the soul itself is the reflection of the higher being, the Spirit or the Monad on its plane. But, as vehicles, we exhibit only a tiny fraction of the experience and the spiritual greatness, power, wisdom and love of the soul. That is why we are still here. The soul's nature is love. The soul's nature and purpose is to serve. We come into incarnation not only for experience; we come in as taking part in a great sacrifice. It is the action of the sacrificial will that brings us into incarnation. The soul makes a sacrifice by reflecting itself on the lower level of dense physical matter. It is an inhibition and a limitation for the soul to be on this level, so always at this level we express a tiny fraction of our true potential. Through the evolutionary process, through the initiatory process, we gradually manifest more and more of the true soul potential: the love nature, the intelligence and eventually the will nature of the soul. Gradually, we become what is known as a soul-infused personality—we become the spiritual being that we all admire so much when we see it. But this is a slow evolutionary process for us, and it is not possible for this total soul-infusing process to take place until a man has completed the third initiation. He is then transfigured. That initiation is called the Transfiguration. He becomes really, truly, a Spiritual Being, a Divine Being, from that point on.

19/3/76

Is it true or not true that all human souls may in fact go through all experience—the experience of Aries, the Piscean experience, and the Aquarian experience—or are certain souls only designated for a particular age?

It depends on the evolution of the soul itself, its point in evolution. Very advanced souls may come into incarnation very infrequently but the vast majority of mankind go through very fast incarnational cycles. Because they need the experience, they have to come in again and again and again. But those of great antiquity and development may have to wait several hundred years until the situation is right for bodies to be created through which they can manifest. There are now coming into incarnation souls who have been out of incarnation for a very long time indeed. They are coming in now under law, under the Plan, and will represent the fore-front of humanity. But most of us incarnate very frequently.

14/2/78

When you were answering that earlier question you mentioned about the souls who were waiting at that time to incarnate. Is mankind unique in the universe? Is there any other humanity in the universe?

Man is everywhere in the universe. Man is a Principle. Man is what occurs when Spirit and Matter come together—and Spirit and Matter are everywhere in the universe. When the Un-created comes into creation, makes the first step into manifestation, when both polarities of Its Being—which we call on the one hand Spirit, and at the furthest pole from that, matter, they are parts of the one whole, of course—when these two meet, at the point of meeting, Man is born. The two Sources, male Spirit and female Matter, produce Man, who is everywhere, not unique to this planet or this system. He is infinite in the universe.

What about his chemical compounds—are they different?

They vary from planet to planet depending on that particular planetary form. The planet Venus is inhabited, so is the planet Mars, but if you went there you would see no one at all, because' they are in etheric matter. If you had etheric vision you would see them.

Have they always been on the etheric physical plane?

No, this is a development. One day this planet, too, will become more and more rarefied, in physical terms, as its matter aspect, through the evolutionary process—and above all through

128

Man's agency—is lifted, occultly raised, and becomes spiritualised. The planet will gradually become what it was at one time, etheric in nature. Before that, of course, Man and the lower kingdoms will exist in forms of subtler and subtler matter. The planet will eventually reach a stage when the dense physical body of man today will be too gross, so that he will function only on the etheric, as he did at one time. It is a process, first, of involution downwards, and then a return, through evolution, back to the Source. Before the Lemurian Race, which was the first truly human race, there were two earlier races which were etheric and were not truly human at all. Now the return journey is being made, only with all the experience and the soul-infusion which has taken place in the meantime—that is the Plan.

So we are really spiritualising matter, occultly lifting up matter. Through our incarnation in matter we are serving the Plan of the Logos. The soul limits itself by its immersion in matter, and brings that matter back to spirit, but with all the experience of being in matter.

Meditation

14/6/77

Is there a particular form of meditation you feel people should follow?

No. There is a meditation for every type of man. I mean, literally, there are hundreds of forms of meditation. For every individual at every level of development; every type of ray structure. For every type of mind and tradition and background there is a meditation; they all vary and one cannot say there is only this way for you given your point in development, with your particular rays, background, training, experience of previous lives, and so on.

Meditation is really a more or less scientific method of bringing about soul contact and eventual soul control. That is, control by the soul of its vehicle, which is the man in incarnation. The meditation, whatever it might be, is the beginning of a process towards that, or a very dynamic result of soul contact and control.

14/6/77

Do you think it is necessary to have guidance on it? It is difficult to know which school to go to.

The thing I would say—it is a difficult question to answer—is subject yourself to a few, perhaps half a dozen ways. Choose what seems right for you—what feels right, what corresponds to your sense of your needs. (I don't mean—which gives you experiences. Most people think that meditation is something you do to get inner experiences. It is not. You may have inner experiences, but they are by the way.) The true purpose of meditation is to bring you into contact and alignment with your soul. Through meditation you build a bridge, a channel of light, between the physical brain and your own soul. The Sanskrit term for it is the Antahkarana. Through the Antahkarana, the energy of the soul pours down into its vehicle. Meditation is to do with the gradual soul-infusing of the individual. You become gradually infused with the energy of your soul, that is the energy of the purpose, the love quality, the intelligence aspect of the soul.

These are aspects of the soul because they are aspects of God. The soul and God are identical. The soul is a part of one great oversoul, which is identical with God. You have within the individual soul, the potential of all Deity. The soul pours its energy down into its vehicle and gradually, step by step—this may take many lives, but it happens, some life has got to be *the* life—the person becomes totally soul-infused. He becomes divine. He stands transfigured. The man is a Diving Being from then on.

8/3/77

Is it necessary for people to meditate in a group?

No, it is not necessary to meditate in a group but it is a most potent form of meditation.

130

The meditation here tonight is, of course, a transmission of energy and there is safety in numbers. For instance, tonight we had the most tremendous energy sent into this room, but safely, because it is shared by a lot of people. Far greater energy can be sent through individuals meditating together than could be sent through these same individuals sitting on their own somewhere.

Their energies could meet but then you would have a group. You are either a group on the physical plane, or a group on the inner plane. Souls are in groups. There is no such thing as a single soul—it is one of a group. This is something which we will come to realise in this coming age; that Hierarchy is a group, humanity is a group. There are only groups of souls. All men are part of a group.

8/3/77

Surely if people can meditate, they still get on the plane of the soul on their own, without the need to be part of a group?

You don't have to be all in one small room, but there is no finer method of meditation than group meditation, because it is only in group formation that the requirements of the new age can be ascertained, can be sensed. It is an age of synthesis we are moving into, of group manifestation. The teachings and the values which will be released into the world, or apprehended and sensed by humanity, will come through group formation and not through individuals as they have done in the past. In the past, some highly evolved or sensitive individual tuned into the cliches, the thought-forms, which are in the mind-belt of the world, put there and energised by the Masters. These individuals put forward the ideas. These worked out through groups and individuals and so were disseminated throughout the world—they became the ideals of any given age. This will change in this coming time, is already beginning to change.

The reappearance of the Christ in Palestine was prepared for by that Disciple who was John the Baptist. Today, the reappearance of the Christ has been prepared for, in a broad sense, by many people, by several millions throughout the world. The

New Group of World Servers is the John the Baptist of today.

It is in group formation that Hierarchy works. This is the way forward for humanity. Likewise with meditation. It is no longer possible, it is no longer right and constructive, for quiet personal development without at the same time the acceptance of the challenge, the duty, of service. Group formation, group meditation and group service is the norm today for aspirants and disciples. The Christ augments all service a thousandfold; for every step one takes towards Hierarchy They take twenty steps towards us. So there is no more potent means of developing yourself than through meditation in group formation. Not that it is impossible otherwise. It is simply better in a group.

10/2/77

When we do this transmission of energies is it really necessary that we shut our eyes?

It is better to shuts one's eyes. It is not necessary. If you are really experienced in this you can talk, write a book or read a book—whichever you do best—chant, write letters, whatever. But if you are not experienced in it you need to concentrate, and in fact, these energies are being transmitted at a very high level indeed and they come and go—there are peaks and troughs. At the peaks you do need to concentrate.

If you concentrate on the centre, the energy follows your thought. This is a fundamental axiom of occultism—that all in the world is energy, and that energy follows thought, conforms itself to thought. So if you place your attention on the ajna centre you draw the energy to this centre, which is the directing centre. It is also the heart centre in the head. Some people say, "I always transmit through the heart centre". This is fine. You cannot transmit through the ajna centre without transmitting through the heart centre. The directing centre is the level at which we should become focused. The majority of people are focused in the solar plexus. They are literally Atlantean in consciousness and the focus of their attention is on the astral level. Modern man should become focused on the mental level, and the governing centre for the mental level is here, the ajna centre, between the eyebrows.

As you do that you find the whole thing lifts. This is the transmuting process. Emotions become governable and transmutable without repression. Repression is harmful but transmutation is essential. The way to transmute the lower emotions and to raise the energy is through meditation, by fixing the attention on certain centres.

I am suggesting that you concentrate on the ajna centre. (It is safe to do it, believe me, I would not say so, if it were not safe. There are centres on which it is not safe to concentrate.) We put the attention on the ajna centre and bring about mental focus.

We have to become mentally focused, it is part of the evolutionary process. Mankind is beginning to think. Gradually, there is a shift in consciousness throughout mankind—obviously, it expresses itself best among the intellectuals, among the more educated peoples of the world, advanced humanity in other words, who are beginning to be more or less polarised mentally. It is only from the ajna centre that you can direct. You cannot direct anything from the solar plexus. You can only react, respond. That is Atlantean consciousness, whereas our Aryan consciousness, at this time, is seated in the ajna centre. We are in process, as part of the Aryan race, of perfecting the mental vehicle.

19/3/76

When you were stressing that the transmission of energy should be unconditioned, not directed towards any specific end, was that because the Will, the Purpose of God is unknown, and therefore we are simply making ourselves available for whatever the purpose might be?

It is simply that these energies from the Hierarchy, from the Christ and the Masters, are already conditioned by certain factors—conditioned by the qualities inherent in the energies themselves, and by the focused minds of the Masters Who are sending them. They know where they are most needed, and in what precise balance and potency, to bring about the desired effect. So we should not send them to any person, group or country in particular, who, we might think, could benefit from these energies. Energy transmission at this level is a very precise scientific process. Only Hierarchy know this science of energy distribution. It is enough that we act as channels.

24/9/76

Could you tell us more about the purpose of meditation for ordinary folk like me, who are beginning to meditate?

The purpose of meditation is to bring one into contact with, and gradual at-one-ment with, one's soul, which is one's true Being. This physical plane personality that we all see when we look in the mirror, is the vehicle for the soul on this plane. But essentially we are a soul, an intelligent spiritual Being on the higher planes, the soul plane. The aim of meditation is to bring the physical brain and the personality on the physical plane, into alignment with that soul, so that a gradual infusion of the personality vehicle by the energy and quality of the soul can take place.

Prayer

23/6/77

I wanted to ask you about prayer now. I mean we do, we pray for help and so on in our daily lives. To whom should we direct prayer?

This depends on who you are and what you are and what you believe. If you are a Christian, then direct your prayer to the Christian idea of God. That might be to God transcendent, outside creation; or as He is, as well as that, inside oneself. God is both, and this is something mankind has to learn in this coming age. One of the major teachings of the Christ will be the fact of God immanent, immanent in all creation, in mankind and all creation; that there is nothing else but God; that we are all part of a great Being. In the case of mankind, a self-conscious aspect of that Being; apparently separate parts, but in fact, totally bound up with every other part of It. And that Being is immanent, everywhere, throughout the whole of space. Space itself is a Being, an Entity.

That aspect of God to which we immediately aspire, can aspire to, is the Logos of our own planet, Who is embodied for us as Sanat Kumara on Shamballa. He is our "Father." God is both within us and can be known—you can see God. In this coming age many, many people will see God, as Sanat Kumara. They will come before Sanat Kumara and take the third Initiation. (Even more will come before the Christ and take the first and second Initiations.) When you take the third Initiation you see God, as Sanat Kumara, the Lord of the World, Who is a real physical Being in etheric matter on Shamballa.

If you are a Buddhist, you might pray to the Buddha to intercede for you.

But we Christians, why not pray to Christ?

Indeed, why not? To whoever is the focus for you. But Christ is not God. He is not coming as God. He is an Embodiment of an aspect of God, the Love aspect of God. He is the embodied soul of all creation. He embodies the energy which is the consciousness aspect of that Being we call God.

But He is so above us that we can only prostrate ourselves and pray to Him, can't we?

You can pray to Him. He would rather, I don't know, but I think He would rather you didn't pray to Him, but to the God within you, which is also within Him. He is simply a better, or clearer manifestation of It than you and me. But if you pray to that God in you, and know that God in you, it is the same God which is in Him.

That seems to me irreverent.

Not at all, this is the fact. He said it Himself. "The Kingdom of God is within you."

I say "you", but I don't mean this little personality you. I mean that Being, which is your true nature. That nature is the same as God, is identical. Man is literally made in the likeness of God. He has to be, because there isn't anything else.

But one can't pray to oneself . . .

One doesn't pray to oneself, one prays to the God within. The thing is to learn to invoke that energy which is the energy of God.

Prayer and worship as we know it today will gradually die out and men will be trained to invoke the power of Deity. This is one reason why the Great Invocation was given out—to enable us to learn the technique of invocation, and to use this in our cyclic Approaches to God at the Three Major Festivals, and also at the nine lesser full-moon Festivals throughout the year.

19/3/76

Is there a connection between meditation and initiation?

The aim of evolution is to become at-one with one's Source; at-one with Divinity, the Logos, or God, one's Spirit, of which the soul on its plane is the reflection. The *immediate* aim of evolution is identification or at-one-ment with the soul; and this is what meditation is for, to bring about this at-one-ment. This leads to Initiation.

It is through the Initiatory process that Liberation takes place. At critical points along this journey man goes through one or other of five Initiations. Many thousands are now standing on the threshold of the first major Initiation, and the coming into the world of the Hierarchy coincides with this unique point in man's development. Millions of people throughout the world, in the next fifty years even, will take the first Initiation.

Aspiration, meditation and service are the factors which lead a man on to the Initiatory Path.

Initiation

18/3/77

Can you give us an indication of the five steps of Initiation?

The Gospel story symbolises them very clearly for us. It does not, of course, show exactly what is required, but it does present humanity, once again, with a story which has been given to mankind over and over again, in many ways, down the ages. This is as old as man—or as old as mid-Atlantean times, when the Initiatory process was brought in to speed up the evolutionary process.

The Birth at Bethlehem, the Birth of Jesus, symbolises for us the birth of the Christ Principle, the Christ Consciousness, in the cave of the heart. When the Christ Consciousness (the energy of the Cosmic Christ, which the Christ, Maitreya, Embodies, anchors on this planet) is lit, as it were, in the human heart, the man can then be prepared for Initiation. That is what is happening in mankind today. The Christ Consciousness is being lit in hundreds of thousands of men and women in the world today; it is manifesting in countless people. It is this fact which is behind the reality of the externalisation, for the first time since Atlantean times, of Hierarchy. They can come into the world now because humanity is prepared. With pain and suffering, the Christ is being born in the human heart. This is the first step into Initiation.

The Christ is the Hierophant at the first two Initiations, and since He will be in the world. He will Initiate men and women into these first two Initiations, outwardly, and in group formation, in the temples of the time.

Some millions are now standing on the very verge of this experience. This is the enormous step forward in evolutionary development which humanity as a whole has taken, and is the opportunity for the Christ to reappear now with the Hierarchy of Masters.

Every Initiation shows control over some level of consciousness—they are all stages of awareness. A plane is really a state of consciousness; when one refers to the physical plane it is in fact to a state of consciousness. When one speaks of the "solar plane" or "cosmic plane", that, again, refers to a state of consciousness.

The First Initiation demonstrates the control over the physical plane. It takes aeons for man to come to this point, and he is brought to it, eventually, by his own soul, through the meditation process. Through meditation, the soul aligns itself with its vehicle—the man in incarnation; the Christ is born and the soul brings its energy to bear on its vehicles, until the man gradually becomes more soul-infused, and eventually takes Initiation.

The Second Initiation is called "The Baptism". It is symbolised by the Baptism of Jesus at Jordan. The Initiate demonstrates his control over the astral plane, over his own astral or emotional nature, which became perfected through the fourth root race, the Atlantean—and which is so powerful in mankind. Most of humanity today are really Atlantean in consciousness. They are focused on the astral plane, their energies work mainly through the solar plexus, and this powerful, sensitive, astral, feeling nature of man, which of course is one of his great achievements, makes it very difficult for him to gain control on this plane. He is swept by the energy of the astral plane—hence the glamour under which mankind lives.

As a result of the shared suffering of humanity in the war, a great deal of the glamour which befogs mankind was lifted, and the Logos Who embodies this planet, underwent, in recent years, a great Cosmic Initiation, which corresponds on cosmic levels to the second Initiation in man. So this planet is being released from glamour to a great degree. The astral plane itself is being lightened, releasing mankind from glamour. It is the development of man, the release of mankind from total control by his astral nature which allows the Logos to take this Initiation.

When the second Initiation is taken, the whole process is speeded up. It takes aeons to come to the first Initiation; it can take several lives to come from that to the second Initiation, which is said to be the most difficult of all the Initiations to take. When that stage has been reached and man controls his astral nature, he then finds himself the subject, not now of glamour, but of illusion—of illusion which is governing his mind. The process from the second to the third Initiation is really the control over the mind and the releasing of himself from illusion. When this process is complete, through the agency of his soul and his Master, he can take the third Initiation—"the Transfiguration". He becomes Divine. The "Transfiguration on the Mount" is the symbol for this.

The Master Jesus (He was then the disciple Jesus) came into the world as a third degree initiate; He did not have to take the first, second, or third Initiation. He went through these processes simply to symbolise them, dramatise them, for us. He did have to take the fourth Initiation, which is called in the West, the "Crucifixion". In the East it is known as "The Great Renunciation", and He went through it in full, physical fact. All initiations take place on the inner planes, are an inner experience; people are not normally crucified—except symbolically—when they take the fourth Initiation. The Disciple Jesus made two great sacrifices: He gave up His body for the use of the Christ, Maitreya, and He underwent this Initiation physically, being crucified in the flesh, to dramatise for us this Great Renunciation. The Initiate has to demonstrate this: that the world of matter no longer has any lure; He has overcome, and can give up everything—family, reputation, talents, life itself—and die the death of his lower nature. All of that is renounced, crucified, for the higher Spiritual Being.

Then comes the great moment of Resurrection, the symbol for the fifth Initiation, which makes one a Master. A Master is a resurrected being. He is someone who has mastered Himself, has mastered His lower nature. He has taken all five of these Initiations and is free, liberated. He has triumphed over matter. Each Initiation is the result of, and also leads to, a great expansion of consciousness. The Masters' consciousness includes the consciousness of the spiritual plane. He has spiritualised His body of manifestation and no longer needs to incarnate on this planet, except by choice, to serve the Plan. He may be asked to do so, by Sanat Kumara, the Lord of the World, as part of the Plan.

The Gospel story is about resurrection. Easter will be one of the three major Spiritual Festivals and Christmas and Good Friday will slowly die out of our consciousness. Resurrection will be the emphasised goal for mankind; resurrection out of matter into Spirit, which makes one a liberated Master.

Telepathy

7/12/76

How do you differentiate between intuition and telepathy?

There is a real difference between telepathy and intuitive perception. There are very many levels of telepathy. Telepathy on a normal human level happens spontaneously, usually through the solar plexus, among all men; among animals for that matter. It is an instinctual, natural means of communication, but it is haphazard. That is an astral type of telepathy. Then there is a mental type of telepathy which again, we all share. All of us are being subjected to, bombarded by, the thoughts of all those around us. We have a screening process which allows us to hear only a certain portion of it, but if a person is sensitive enough he can tune into all sorts of nonsense which is going on all the time. Most of us have experience of a voice coming in, like a telephone conversation, which is someone else's, and you have a sense of the distance involved.

Telepathy as used by the Hierarchy is of a different order. It is used, again, on different levels. Where it is used to contact a disciple who is impressable, but is not conscious of a subjective contact, the Master simply impresses the brain of the disciple through his (the disciple's) soul. That disciple will have a connection to Hierarchy through his soul group; he will be either on the outskirts of, or more central to, a Master's Ashram on the inner planes. He will have some connection to a Master, and through his soul and his relation to the group soul he will be impressable on mental levels. He may be totally unaware of the source of the information. He may simply do things without even knowing that he is receiving impressions at all. This is possible. It happens all the time. There is a more conscious

140

level of that, where the disciple has a very conscious relationship to his own soul. He can bring the energy from the soul on to the physical plane, into the brain. There is an alignment between the physical brain and the soul. It is through that channel that the Master deliberately "telepaths"—transmits—a message which is consciously received by the disciple.

There has to be similarity of vibration to bring it about, to make contact possible. When there is some analogous vibration and a need—there also has to be the need—the Master may stimulate the contact to such a point that the disciple becomes consciously aware that he is receiving specific information, and he may then go even further and be used in a specific way, for instance by overshadowing by the Master. Overshadowing is a normal means of contact, which is still to do with the Science of Impression. It is a great science, which ranges from the merest astral or solar plexus impression to the highest buddhic level and total overshadowing, as in the case of the disciple Jesus by the Christ.

Intuitive perception on the other hand, stems directly from the buddhic level of the man himself, via his own soul. That can happen without the agency of a Master at all. The energy can flow, and perceptions, intuitive truths, and so on, can be ascertained, but they will tend to be broad and generalised in their nature, and not specific and detailed as to the Plan. Various broad, general aspects of information about the regeneration of mankind, and so on, is coming to mediums and sensitives all over the world. The world is now flooded with information of this kind; some of it from the highest levels, the intuitive levels, some of it from the lower psychic levels. You have to discriminate between the different levels. At its highest it is inspiration.

24/5/77

Is it possible to develop this higher telepathy or is it just a gift?

It is certainly possible. There is no doubt that in this coming time this will be the normal mode of communication between men at a certain stage of development. Gradually, in this coming age, speech will die out as a means of communication. We shall telepath. This will become the norm between people at the same stage of development.

Telepathy is a fact in nature. It is a normal development of mankind. All the animals communicate telepathically, in an instinctual fashion, through the solar plexus. But the telepathy I am talking about is a development of the higher mind. It is through the soul, and then it is not unconscious. It is under the control of two minds, and is a conscious, controlled communication between two minds which might be thousands of miles apart.

A shift in consciousness is taking place from astral consciousness to mental consciousness. This is bringing humanity to the very verge of Initiate consciousness. As we become mentally polarised, so the faculty of telepathy can be unfolded. It unfolds spontaneously as we develop a magnetic aura.

All groups should seek to develop telepathy in this coming time because although the Masters will be in the world, They will still use telepathy as Their major mode of contact, especially when dealing with disciples and aspirants.

5/3/76

Is this higher telepathy a conscious state or a trance state?

It is not a trance state, no. It is a question of focusing the mind on a higher centre and being able to keep it there. It is a fully conscious, controlled process.

Psychic Powers

4/4/78

Do you therefore anticipate, as a result of this implication, that the great world religions, like Buddhism and Christianity, will be more sympathetic towards, and more aware of the significance of, the development of psychic skills and the whole psychic area. I mean, from the little I know of Buddhism and Christianity, they don't seem terribly aware or into, the psychic area. Would you agree with that?

Yes, I think so, inevitably. When the Masters are in the world, openly in the world, when the Christ has declared Himself—and if humanity responds in the correct way—the whole process of transformation which is taking place will speed up. Inevitably, the religions of the world like Christianity and Buddhism will begin to accept the reality of psychic energy. Psychic energy is the primal force in the world. It is the energy of creation itself. Under a controlled mind it creates and destroys. Whole worlds are created by psychic energy; worlds are destroyed by this energy. The fact that we are sitting here, that you are listening to me and I am listening to you, tonight, is the result of the use of psychic energy by that great Being who ensouls this planet—whom we call the Logos. It is His concentrated use of psychic energy that makes us at all. We are thoughts in His mind. If He decided, by another manifestation of psychic energy, to destroy that thoughtform, we would automatically and instantaneously be destroyed. That is the power of psychic energy.

More and more, as the New Age unfolds, as man's inner mental capacities unfold, he will become aware of the tremendous power of psychic energy. Our manifestations of it today are as nothing. In this New Age mankind will, by an act of the will, by his mental control of psychic energy, create machines which he will programme to create the artifacts of our civilisation, and leave time and energy to involve himself in, and explore, his own nature; know what he is—to develop and express what he is as a great manifesting Son of God. The Masters can do this because They have released the awareness which gives one the power over psychic energy. It is a question of awareness. It is an expansion of conscious awareness to include progressively, ever higher and higher levels of energy manifestation.

Sorry, I don't quite understand why the Masters can do that?

They can do that because Their awareness includes awareness and *control* on all planes open to us on this planet, including the spiritual.

5/5/77

Do Initiates have "second-sight"—certain abilities—and how do they know they are Initiates?

143

There are many Initiates of the first degree who don't know they are Initiates. If, for instance, you took Initiation in a previous life, you could quite well not know you were an Initiate; you would not necessarily remember it. But if you became an Initiate in any given life it would be an experience which you would not doubt. It would be so extraordinary, so overwhelming, that you would not be able to experience it and not know about it.

Initiates don't necessarily have "second-sight". These psychic gifts, psychic unfoldments, may or may not follow spiritual development. They can be "sat" for. I mean you can develop psychic faculties, and that has nothing to do with spiritual development at all; and some of those using the psychic powers, especially the lower psychic powers, most actively, may well have little spiritual development, relatively speaking; they are really manifesting ancient, Atlantean, forms of consciousness. These powers may go hand in hand with spiritual development; sometimes they do, and sometimes they don't. So the fact of a man or woman being an Initiate is no guarantee of their having "second-sight", being clairvoyant, having etheric vision, or being clairaudient or telepathic. Likewise, the existence of clairvoyance or clairaudience, and so on, is no indication that that person is Initiate.

4/4/78

Is the aura part of the etheric?

All the energies work through the etheric. The energy from the mental plane—there are four mental planes—the energy from the seven astral planes, plus the energy from the four etheric planes, all manifest in and through the etheric. The etheric is the vital body through which the energies from all the planes flow—so the aura is made up of all of that. If the person is strongly contacting his soul, it will have within it energy from the soul plane. It will have energy from the mental planes, from whatever level he is contacting, drawing it; energy from the astral planes, inevitably. And of course, all of this is flowing through the ocean of etheric energy in which we live. Our

144

etheric body is just a more individualised part of an ocean of etheric energy which is everywhere in the planet.

Our soul takes part of that and creates the etheric man. Where the streams of energy cross, vortices or centres are formed which are linked to the endocrine system and through that govern the physical body. Our physical body is a precipitation of the etheric counterpart and so is linked to everything else through it. We are totally connected with the etheric plane of the world. The vibrations of these centres are what creates the aura of man, and the etheric body conditions it.

4/4/78

What is etheric vision?

If a person has etheric vision it means that he is able to see at least some of the four planes of the etheric physical—i.e. of the physical planes above the dense physical. There are seven physical planes, four of them being finer than the gaseous physical. They are of a finer and finer form of matter, which to most people is invisible. Unless we have etheric vision—it is really a double focus—we don't see it, but in certain circumstances, for instance in a darkened room, we may see the energy streaming off a person, or we may see a field of luminous grey-blue light around the person, the etheric body. It is the exact counterpart of the physical body. In the womb, the etheric body is laid down before the physical baby which is really a precipitation downwards from it. If we have etheric vision, therefore, we see one or more of these four planes of matter.

Healing in the Future

28/2/78

When the Christ is working in the world will He in any way work as a healer as Jesus did?

Yes, but only in a private capacity. Not in the same public,

145

magical way to demonstrate Himself as the Christ. Not that; He will not perform the miracles. These miracles are now being performed by men and women in the world all the time. He said then: "These things that I do, you shall do also and greater things than these, because I go to the Father." "Going to the Father" means He went to Shamballa. He has come into a closer at-one-ment with the Will aspect and not only the love aspect, of God.

He is a greater Avatar, and He has been able to release into the world, as the Christ, for the last 2,000 years, the energy which has made it possible for mankind to develop the Christ Consciousness. It is this which has enabled them to perform what at that time were called miracles, which today are called spiritual or esoteric healing. Daily, all over the world, there are miracles of healing performed.

The Masters will institute Healing Centres, and train Initiates and Disciples, who will be doctors of all kinds, in groups. These groups will be made up of orthodox doctors, surgeons, homoeopaths, acupuncturists, radionic practitioners. Colour and sound therapy will be used; the groups will have spiritual healers, and someone with etheric vision to advise on the state of the etheric body and centres.

They will work as a team.

22/3/77

Could you say something about the new form healing will take?

The health of any individual depends on the correct and free flow of energy in its etheric system (its counterpart body, or etheric envelope—of which the dense physical body is a precipitation. The etheric comes first. The soul magically brings together an etheric structure which in the womb precipitates and become the baby.) from all sources—from the soul and from every plane of energy. The etheric system is connected with the etheric plane of the planet.

We are all interconnected. We are all part of the earth, from our dense physical and etheric physical nature. Through this etheric physical body flow all the energies of which we are made. It has seven major centres connected to the spine of the physical body and to the seven major endocrine glands—the correspondence of these centres on the physical plane. The health of the body depends entirely on the correct functioning and relationship of these glands, as we are beginning to discover. The correct functioning of the glands depends on the correct flow of energy from the etheric centres and therefore on the correct flow of energy coming into the etheric body from whatever source. Most disease is caused by the wrong use or mis-use of soul energy. This depends on the stage of evolution of the person; whether they are misusing soul energy or whether they are tapping too great a stream of astral energy from the astral plane; or perhaps there are soul energies flowing in which are not actually manifesting through service.

The soul demands service of its vehicle, and it brings it into incarnation as a part of its sacrificial service. This is really why we are in incarnation—not just to learn. The fundamental reason why we are here is because we have made a sacrifice. As great spiritual Beings, through an act of the spiritual will, we have sacrificed ourselves by coming into matter. That is the true basis of rebirth, or reincarnation. This way we serve the Plan. In order to serve the Plan we have to do it cyclically, and the soul brings together again and again a new body, and presents you with certain opportunities and experiences. The wrong use of any energy, the wrong flow, or a damning up of energy at any point in the etheric, works out eventually on the physical plane as illness of some kind or another. There develops an inflammation caused by too great an energy flow at some point; there is a stasis; or else there is a depletion, just not enough energy of the correct type flowing in through the centre to the gland. Therefore it is inhibited in its action and the result is illness.

All healing, all spiritual healing, takes place on the etheric level. All esoteric healing is done through the etheric envelope, and this gradually works out on to the physical plane. True esoteric healing is to do with the transformation of the man, not of the body at all. You change the man and therefore you change the energy flow and the result is balance, equilibrium, health.

147

As George Ohsawa, who brought Macrobiotics to the West, said: "It is easy to cure the disease. What is difficult is to cure the man." You have to change the man to change the disease, otherwise it will turn into some other kind of disease. What the healer does is transform the flow of energy in the system. This works out as temporary or, if you can change the man, permanent change.

In this coming time the human evolution will come closer to the deva or angelic evolution (and the Christ is bringing some very high devas into the world with Him). Also of course, the Masters, all of Them, work with the deva evolution.

A Master calls on certain healing devas—the violet devas for instance—and they pour their energy, their vitality, into the patient through the etheric system and the healing results. These devas will come closer (and in fact are now coming closer to humanity), will work very closely with us, and will teach us how to keep the vital, etheric body in equilibrium; the art of tuning into and living off the prana of the air, direct from the sun, so that we shall actually eat less food. I don't say all will but the more advanced will.

Through the relationship to the devic kingdom and through the association with the higher devas, we shall eventually get rid of all disease on the planet. They will teach us to heal through sound and through colour. They respond to sound: to call a deva you utter a certain mantram and the deva comes in response to it. This is why, of course, the use of mantrams is very carefully guarded, because you can call on devas of realms below the human which are very dangerous indeed. A lot of havoc is caused in this way by misuse, wrong use, or partial knowledge.

Of course, even in the short term, as mankind uses the energies flowing through his etheric envelope more correctly as a result of the changed conditions on earth: the reduction of tension and fear; greater leisure; new meaning and impetus to life; the health of mankind will improve enormously.

Fear of Death

28/2/78

Why is man so afraid of death; will this attitude change in future?

Man approaches death with the idea that he is vanquished, lost for ever, and it is this sense that his identity is going to be obliterated which terrifies him. Did he realise that this identity, this consciousness, was an immortal Being, and that on the other side of the gate through which we pass at death, he would stand in a new and clearer light, aware in an altogether greater sense of his identity; meeting again those whom he had known on the physical plane before; and also becoming gradually aware of further and higher aspects of his Being of which till then he had been unaware, he would approach death quite differently.

Compared with the experience of birth, man's exit from this world can be, and should be, painless indeed. But few know this, and hence the fear. In this coming time the Masters and Their Disciples will teach the truth about this experience we call death, and man will wait serenely and hopefully for its call. When this knowledge becomes general, a great new freedom will become open to men. They will see life for what it is, as a stage in an unending journey, and death itself as a further and less limiting experience on that road. So man will conquer the fear of death. When his physical body loses its usefulness he will willingly, gladly, surrender it, restore it to the earth. Death is fundamentally restitution. Through the Law of Rebirth he will return to this plane to carry further his soul's purpose.

What happens in the process of dying? What are the steps or stages?

First, through the centre through which he is normally focused, depending on his level of development, his etheric, vital body exits. This can be very fast indeed, but normally takes some time. A full three days should be allowed before the body is buried or cremated; the latter is the only hygienic method of disposal, and will become the norm.

Gradually, the etheric sheath is dissipated, returns to the

etheric ocean in which we exist, and man is left in his subtler astral and mental sheaths, which in their turn are likewise slowly restored to their origin.

The Tibetan teaching, in *The Book of the Dead*, holds that man spends forty days in what is called the Bardo, and the aim is to get through that period more quickly if possible. They give precise instructions to follow lights of various intensity to avoid the magnetic pull back into incarnation. One should aim to follow the brightest light. In practice, the last reflex of the nerves at the moment of dying should be used to carry one's consciousness to the highest level; this is dependent on the tension created by one's aspiration. The dying should be left in peace to create this tension, helped by loving friends or the trained help of the priest or minister who understands these rites; this of course, is not always the case.

When a man awakens on the other side, he sees both ways: he sees the life and forms of the plane on which he now finds himself, and those of the plane he has just left. He is less alone, less separated, than he ever is at birth. Friends and helpers are there to guide him and ease his journey upward through the planes, should that be his destiny.

Suffering

6/1/77

When you were speaking about the intense suffering that's going on all over the world, did you mean that the Christ is coming to alleviate that suffering, to prevent many people from dying?

I am not saying He must come now *only* to stop suffering. His decision to come *now* is to help, by His Presence in the world, to speed up the process of change, so that the suffering will be relieved. But we still have to make the changes.

This may sound very unsympathetic, it's not meant to be, could it not be that this suffering seems worse now than in the past, simply because there's more of it? It's not worse suffering—there are just more people suffering; and surely they will get through their suffering, die and perhaps come back in different circumstances. Why is it so important for their suffering to be terminated?

The reason is the creation of the *one* humanity, the idea of the one humanity. This, above all, is the Plan of the Christ. Mankind itself is beginning to sense itself as One; in this coming time it will be One. It is our next step forward in evolution. Brotherhood isn't simply an ideal which we might or might not have. It is a fact in nature; only we haven't manifested it yet. In this coming time it is our destiny, the Will of God, to manifest this fact. All the activity and guidance of the Hierarchy will be bent towards this end. This can only come through *right relationship*. It is to bring about right relationships between men, first, that the Christ is coming; right relationship to God and to one another. If one man is starving in a world of plenty you do not have right relationship. If 500 million people are starving in such a world then you certainly do not have right relationship. It is not a spiritual activity to let someone else die of starvation when you have more than enough food. It is to cleanse the planet of this disease of separatism, to create right relationships, that He comes.

A great deal of the suffering which humanity undergoes is totally unnecessary. It is inflicted by man on man. The Christ will show that it is essential that this needless suffering by millions must cease; the exploitation of man by his brother must cease, in order to restore balance and sanity to the world.

Education in the Future

30/8/77

How will education differ in the future?

The educational systems we need for humanity must be built on the inner truth that man is a soul, manifesting on this plane as a personality. Education must be geared to that truth and not to the cramming into children's minds of information which will

151

fit them as cogs into an obsolete machine. I am not saying that we shall not make artifacts, not at all. But we have to learn to live more simply.

Children will be recognised as souls in incarnation governed by certain specific Rays or streams of energy, on five levels: the soul, the persisting Ray energy; the personality, which energy changes from life to life; the three vehicles of the personality, the mental, astral/emotional and physical bodies, each of which can be on different Rays. A knowledge of the child's point in evolutionary development will be the first essential. This can be ascertained scientifically by reference to the development, more or less, of the chakras or force centres in the etheric body.

Great attention will be paid to the creation, through meditation, of the channel of Light, the antahkarana, between the brain and the soul, as well as the intensive development and rounding out of the child's lower, concrete mind. In this way a balanced approach to life, objective and subjective, will be inculcated. The teaching of universal ideas and history will encourage the growth of international identification and citizenship. A sense of personal responsibility for the welfare of others and a definite stimulation of the love nature will likewise be foremost in the new approaches to Education.

The present dichotomy between religion and science will be healed, and through the recognition and study of psychic energy and its manifestations, a more correct application of science can be made, a science accessible to more varied types of men. The present extreme specialisation will go, to some extent.

Effect on the Lower Kingdoms

27/1/76

You talk a lot about the Masters being of service to men, which brings me to a very simple thing, which is—do you think that man is here for the planet or that the planet is here for man?

152

I think that man is here as part of a total Whole, which includes all kingdoms in nature. Man's role, man's true function on the planet, is to act as a sorting house of energies and to scientifically transmit these energies to the lower kingdoms in nature. In this way he becomes a co-worker with the Logos. This is the true destiny of man—when he knows himself as the divine being he is and can utilise the divine energies streaming through Shamballa from the solar system and beyond. He can consciously control these forces, control and direct; and raise, occultly lift up, the lower kingdoms in nature. So man has a very important part to play in the planet, but he is only one aspect, one kingdom. It is a very important one because he is the midway point between spirit and matter; both meet in him. He is also the Macrocosm of the sub-human kingdoms.

30/8/77

I wonder how the Christ's coming will affect the other kingdoms:—the animal, the vegetable and the mineral?

Tremendously. Not so much the Christ—or shall we say, not only the Christ—but the Christ will gradually evoke in mankind the ability to see itself as a part of the Whole, responsible for the lower kingdoms.

There is a Plan for all the kingdoms in nature, and there are Masters Who have nothing to do with the human kingdom at all, but Whose total concern are the other kingdoms; or the deva or angel evolution. There are only a certain number of Masters Who concern Themselves with the human evolution. We imagine that we are the only ones who count. The evolution of the lower kingdoms will be greatly stimulated as Man himself evolves, and quickly now, with Hierarchy returning to the everyday world.

28/6/77

What of the other forms of life on this planet?

As the Masters help us to develop self-consciousness, so They help the lower kingdoms to develop consciousness. Each king-

153

dom depends on the kingdom immediately above it for its evolutionary stimulus. The animal kingdom depends for its development and the stimulus to its intelligence nature on the mind of man.

Gradually, in the first place through the domesticated animals—those animals who work and live most closely with man—the whole of the animal kingdom is being stimulated mentally, through man's mind. Through the animal kingdom, the vegetable kingdom is being perfected—by going through the process of being eaten by the animals and lifted into a higher kingdom.

The mineral kingdom receives its energy from the sun, through the various planets through Shamballa, through the Hierarchy, through the human kingdom. The human kingdom acts as a sorting house through which the higher energies flow to perfect the lower kingdoms. So there is a very real and reciprocal relationship existing between mankind and the lower kingdoms. Gradually, in this coming age—it is already beginning to happen, you can see it growing in consciousness—mankind will come to realise its relation to the lower kingdoms and their dependence on humanity. A new relationship will develop between the human and the other kingdoms.

30/9/76

Could I just ask you the part animals play in this evolutionary process?

They have a very great part, of course, like all the kingdoms in nature. Each kingdom grows out of the other. The first to be laid down was the mineral kingdom. Out of that grew the vegetable kingdom, out of that the animal kingdom and from that grew the human. Out of the human kingdom is growing the Spiritual Kingdom—the "kingdom of souls", or the "Kingdom of God"—which is the Hierarchy.

Eighteen and a half million years ago, in middle Lemurian times, early animal-man had reached a relatively high stage of development: he had developed a strong physical body; a co-ordinated astral or emotional feeling body; and the germ

154

of mind, incipient mind, which could form the nucleus of a mental body. At that point the Logos of our planet took physical manifestation as Sanat Kumara, the Lord of the World, on Shamballa. The Centre we call Shamballa was formed.

With Sanat Kumara, from Venus, came the Lords of the Flame, Who brought that energy we call Mind. This energy stimulated the incipient mind of early animal-man and the Individualisation of Man took place.

The human egos or souls on their plane, the highest mental plane, who were waiting for this very point in time to take incarnation, made that very sacrifice and came into incarnation for the first time. The human evolutionary journey began.

30/9/76

What happens to animals now? Do they evolve?

Animals at the moment are evolving through the agency of man. They are responding to the energy of mind—the fifth principle of mind—which is radiated to them by man. In this way, their incipient intelligence is gradually being stimulated. You see this working out in the animals that live with man—the domesticated animals. Gradually, there is a dying out of the ancient wild animals like the rhinoceros, and so on. The domesticated animals are becoming more and more intelligent by responding to man's mind. Eventually, you will see experiments where animals will manifest certain mediumistic faculties through the agency of the human mind.

Later, but several millions of years ahead, the gate to Individualisation (animals no longer become human) closed in mid-Atlantean times, will be opened again and animals will individualise. At the moment animals have no self-conscious soul. They are part of a generic soul. When a cat dies it is merged into one soul. It loses whatever identity it had on the physical plane in that group soul which is Cat. This is true in a certain sense of man, but in man there is also individuality. That individualisation occurred for man in Lemurian days.

Part of the world consciousness has expressed itself by certain people trying to hang on to forms of animal and plant life through various preservation societies that have sprung up over the last couple of years. Surely this is being presumptuous on the part of man, to hang on to a form of life which has outgrown its usefulness; and the souls embodied in these forms clearly must have passed on to some better form in which to be incarnated. Or is it something that is an educational process? Does it actually fit into the Plan?

When an animal species dies out—and many are dying out, as we know—this is a result of certain great energies. The great destructive energy of the First Ray of Will or Power, is causing tremendous havoc in the animal kingdom.

5/3/76

Is this destructive?

It is destructive and intentional. The old forms are destroyed in order to make way for the new forms—better, finer forms. You can't destroy life. You can only destroy form, which is renewable at a higher level. Life is indestructible. It doesn't matter, except to a sentimentalist, that the white rhinoceros or whatever, dies out. My personal view is that it's not a bad thing to have a few in zoos as a reminder of our prehistoric past; but they are fundamentally prehistoric animals and are dying out. Great numbers of animals have died out and will continue to, by the actions of the First Ray in its destroyer aspect.

Of course, man is accelerating this process unnaturally by his greedy hunting of these animals; in the case of the rhino for a spurious aphrodisiac thought to come from its horn.

FREE-WILL

24/1/78.

If a figure like the Christ Himself were to appear and speak in this way people would really do things because it was Him and not out of their own freedom, wouldn't they?

Yes. Although He is emerging in the country where He is—and He is emerging very soon—He is not immediately going to declare Himself.

You are talking about free-will. Hierarchy and the Christ never, under any circumstances, infringe our free-will. One of the reasons why the Christ, although in the world, is not at this moment speaking on radio or television to the world, or to the United Nations, is because He in no sense wants to infringe human free-will. He is in total agreement, shall we say, with what you have just said. He is aware of the danger that many would follow Him simply because He is the Christ. When the Christ emerges, but before He has declared Himself, many people will follow Him even though they may not know He is the Christ; whether they know He is the Christ or not. Those who know what to look for may recognise Him.

Those who don't know what to look for, or are not prepared that He has come into the world—and this depends on the success of the preparation being made for Him now—won't necessarily associate the man who is the Christ with the Christ. They may follow Him simply because they believe in what He stands for. This is the essential thing. Those who follow the Christ for what He stands for, whether they recognise Him as the Christ or not, will find automatically flowing through them—when they put these ideals which He is expressing into effect in their everyday lives—His energy—the energy of the Cosmic Christ, the True Spirit of the Christ. That will flow to

157

them and He will work through them. He can change the world through them.

If He were today, tomorrow, to get up and say: "I am the Christ", many people would believe Him. He is such an extraordinary man that many people would believe He was the Christ, and in an emotional way would give Him their allegiance. They would follow Him because they knew He was the Christ, not because they were ready for the renunciations which He will call for. He will call for sacrifice, renunciations, so that all men may share the produce of the world. Those who are not ready for that won't follow the Christ—even if they recognise Him. Those who are ready for that will follow the Christ, even though they don't recognise Him as the Christ. But they have to believe in what He is saying for themselves, not because He is the Christ. So there will be a period between His Emergence and His declaration of His true status, to enable mankind to make its choice and take the first steps into sharing.

Others will ignore Him completely and go on in their old selfish ways. The coming of the Christ does not mean that overnight all mankind will suddenly become unselfish. Selfishness is something that mankind has to grow out of. It is a stage. It is a stage in the evolutionary process. There are today millions of *unselfish* men and women in the world, who are ready for the change, ready for sharing, ready for the sacrifices that sharing means.

24/1/78

Does the idea of a Plan not infringe our free-will?

The Christ and the Masters are not going to do anything but show the way. They are not going to build the new age. We have to build it. We have still to make the inner changes. We have still to make the decisions of *accepting* the Plan. The Christ and the Masters will show that there exists a Plan—a Plan which issues from God, from the Centre which we call Shamballa where the Will of God is known. They are the custodians of this Plan, the Agents of the Plan. But it has to work out through man, on the physical plane. There will be no coercion at all. What you must not forget is that Hierarchy is a continuum. There is the Christ and there are the Masters. But then there are also the fourth, third, second and first degree Initiates; and all the disciples and aspirants on the fringes of Hierarchy—and *they are humanity*. Hierarchy does not stop with the Masters. (If you like, in a technical sense, it stops with the first degree Initiates.)

The Initiates and disciples are the ones who are putting the Plan into effect; through whom the Christ and the Masters are working and will work. They are the builders of the new age, not only the Christ and the Masters. They can point the way, but the actual new age structures, political, economic, financial, social, and so on, will all be built by the trained Initiates and disciples of the Hierarchy, men and women in the world. They are not contravening human free-will, because they are humanity.

24/1/78

What I was speaking about was something subtler.

I see and I sense, I think, your query, your problem, your worry; but I can assure you that there is nobody more concerned with preserving the free will of mankind than Hierarchy. They never infringe our freewill on any pretext. However pleasant or attractive it might be to us that They should interfere, They never do. Everything has to work through man. Where They can interfere—a kind of interference, if you like—is through the impressing of the minds of Their disciples. But they are men and women in the world, and also in Hierarchy, so there is no interference. Through These disciples the Plan works out.

Christianity was really built by St. Paul. The Christ, working through Jesus, inaugurated the Piscean Age and with it the Christian religion, but the structure of Christianity, of the Church, was built by St. Paul—and St. Paul made a number of mistakes. He distorted Christianity considerably. He is now one of the Masters of the Wisdom, the Master Hilarion (and He

159

is one of Those who will soon be in the world), but He made these mistakes, and He wasn't prevented from making these mistakes.

No disciple is ever prevented from making mistakes. He makes the mistakes, humanity suffers through the mistakes, so the Plan suffers through the mistakes, but the Plan eventually works out. The Plan is the ideal. It stems from Shamballa in its ideal form. It is brought to the Hierarchy in the first place by the Buddha, Who is on Shamballa, and the three Great Lords—the Christ, the Manu and the Lord of Civilisation, at the head of the three Departments in the Hierarchy—resolve which part of the Plan can be put into effect in the immediate 100 years or 1,000 years, or whatever. The Lord of Civilisation's task, as a kind of Managing Director, is to approximate that Plan to the possible. The Plan is the ideal for mankind—to release the energies, the ideas, into the mind-belt. Mankind responds to them. But it is always an approximation to the ideal, and if it meant infringing human free will to make sure the Plan worked out, it would not be done.

I see that.

It is up to us. It is always up to us and it still will be up to us.

I think it is best to discern the ideals as well.

Of course. This is how They work. But where do these ideals come from, do you think? Where does the ideal of brotherhood come from? From where do you think the ideas come which are now beginning to govern men's minds? Do you think they drop from the sky or suddenly emerge from men's minds? No, they are *sent* into the mind-belt by Hierarchy. They are put there as thought-forms.

Then the sensitive minds of the race respond to these thought-forms. We have a great idea. We discover atomic energy. Or we discover that the world is round, or whatever. These are discoveries which are made by initiate disciples, responding to thought forms which have already been placed in the mind-belt by the Hierarchy.

What happens to our free-will?

Man has free-will. He has limited free-will and nothing happens to it. What has happened up to now is that he has given it full reign and mankind has made many mistakes, and suffered, through the indulgence of its free-will. Man has limited free-will to withstand the evolutionary force—the great cosmic sweep of evolution—for a time. This planet is part of a system, of a greater Entity, the Logos of this Solar System. Our planet is a centre in the body of that Entity, and the evolution of our Earth is related to the evolution of the system. Our free-will is limited to the extent that we are allowed to withstand that evolutionary force for so long and no longer. Sooner or later, willy-nilly, we are swept by the force of evolution, by the great cosmic magnet, back into line with the Will of God.

What is happening today, for the first time since early Atlantean times, is that mankind's freewill and the Will of God as it is known on Shamballa, are coming into correct alignment. The three great centres, Shamballa, Hierarchy and Humanity are now in a more correct alignment than they have ever been, because for the first time for untold thousands of years, man's free-will is becoming the same as God's will. When man's free-will is different from God's will, man has difficulty, has problems and suffering. But when man's free-will, which remains free-will, is by *his own free choice* brought into line with Divine Will, all is well. We have always had the possibility to make a divine existence, a beautiful world, without suffering, simply by bringing our free-will out of alignment with our own personal predilections, our own personal desire nature, and into alignment with our soul purpose, which is divine purpose.

As we gradually grow, become more and more a soul-infused personality, exhibiting more and more of our true soul purpose, so we bring our human will, which is still our own free will, into line with the Divine Will—the Plan and Will which the Logos of this planet has for us. We are really thoughts in the mind of the creating Logos. As we bring our exterior lives into line with that Plan which He has for us as creations of Himself, all is well,

161

mankind does not suffer, we build right human relationships—between man and man and between man and God. Where we express only our separative free-will, our sense of ourselves as separate entities, selfishly oriented, there the trouble starts. Always, sons of men have become Sons of God and brought their own little separate will into line with the Divine Will. They have become Initiates and eventually Masters. This has happened through all the centuries. Today, for the first time in human history, mankind *as a whole* can do the same thing.

POLITICAL EFFECTS

The Three Disasters

21/12/76

Information made available to us about the previous change-over of Ages seems to indicate not only just enormous upheaval, but also an enormous physical upheaval of the planet itself. Is this true?

The incidence of earthquakes will be seen to have been mounting in intensity and frequency for the last 150 years, and is now reaching a climax; now barely a month goes by without a major earthquake somewhere in the world. The incidence of earthquakes and catastrophic activity—disaster—has been mitigated greatly by the invocation of the Avatar of Synthesis into the world, bringing about synthesis and fusion; and by the energy of the Spirit of Peace, bringing about the transformation and the transmutation of the lower to the higher. Without this intervention, these disasters would be of an intensity far greater than anything we know.

Mankind has come through, in this century, one of the greatest disasters it has ever known: the great war from 1914–1945, which from the Hierarchical point of view, was one war. In it, many millions died and we are still suffering from its effects. Large areas of the planet were devastated, and social life was destroyed to an extraordinary extent. It was a precipitation on to the physical plane of a war which has been going on, on the inner planes, on the astral and mental levels, since Atlantean times, when it brought about the destruction of the Atlantean continent. It was a major disaster and a major experience for mankind.

Mankind is facing, though many in the world today are unaware of the fact, another major disaster, which is the disaster of famine. Today we have 460–500 million people literally

163

starving to death, in a world of plenty. If this isn't a "major disaster", I don't know what is!

But because it is not happening around us, we ignore the fact. The extraordinary thing about humanity is that millions of its own kind—its own common humanity—can be dying of starvation, suffering hunger, malnutrition and disease without our noticing it as a major catastrophe. So these two great disasters have faced us in present times, plus the incidence of earthquakes.

The Christ is now returning imminently to the world to act as the Agent of Divine Intervention, in such a way that He can mitigate the effects of these disasters to a certain extent—disasters which would otherwise cause widespread hardship and suffering. The major reason for the Christ's return *now* is to prevent the catastrophe of famine from engulfing more millions. Much of the world today faces starvation; hundreds of millions will starve and die in the coming years, unless we set into motion the process of sharing. It is for this reason more than any other that the Christ has brought forward the date of His return to the world. There is another reason—the response of humanity to this spiritual outflow of energies is, as to everything else, cyclic in nature. We are on an upward wave of response, and the Christ hopes that by coming now He can take advantage of this upward wave while it lasts, to inaugurate the era of Goodwill, of sharing, and of right relationship, before we go down into a trough again. These are the major factors behind the *imminent* return of the Christ.

In May 1976 there occurred an event of enormous significance to the world. These energies of the Christ, and the Hierarchy in general, emanate from the buddhic level, almost exclusively from that level, and therefore have to be stepped down—losing potency at every point of the stepping-down process. Since May 1976 the Christ has released into the world a great Blessing.

He has brought forward the date of His return so much that there is no longer time to prepare the way for Him, to prepare men's minds for His Coming; so He is having to do it Himself. He is releasing now, the energy of the Avatar of Synthesis and

164

the Spirit of Peace; of the Buddha; His own Love Ray, no longer simply from the buddhic plane but down through the planes: through the four mental planes, the seven astral planes, down on to the lowest of the four etheric planes. The effect now is *as if* the Christ were physically present in the world. They are being released at their maximum potency. It is altogether new, and means that these energies which until now have been only partial in their effect, and therefore slow, are now acting directly and potently, and will bring about changes which until now have appeared impossible.

Even in the coming months and years you will see extraordinary happenings in the world. There will be no doubt in your mind that the Christ is coming. People will come together; nations will come into new alignments; groups which up to now have been at one another's throats will suddenly find that they are friends, able to compromise and come together. Certain areas of the world like the Middle East, like Belfast, South America and Africa, will settle down into a new kind of peaceful orderliness. The chaos, the disturbance, will gradually die down and men will be able to give their minds to the New Order, the new Dispensation, the new structures, and quickly put them into effect under the impression of the Christ. *He will be in the world literally in the next few months.* The energies are doing His work for Him, ahead of His Presence. This is unique, and it is a great Blessing, released to prepare men, to show that He is actually on His way. Permission to release this Blessing was given by the Lord of the World Himself, Sanat Kumara on Shamballa.

You don't have to know the date of His coming. Soon everyone will know for themselves that the Christ has come. The changes taking place will be so amazing that you will know that something is happening—that the Christ has come. Others may not know exactly what is taking place, but they, too, will realise that something quite extraordinary is happening. And when you see this man working in a certain way, releasing His energy, you must surely know that this is the Christ.

Give Him your allegiance. Allow Him to work through you.

"Catastrophe Complex"

Author's Note: There is prevalent today what I call a "catastrophe complex". From all sides, prognostications of disaster are being given out. I consider it necessary to counter this destructive fear syndrome—for that is largely what it is. There *is* catastrophe today—millions are starving to death in a world of plenty; the incidence of earthquakes is lessening, due to the Presence of the Christ—He acts as the Agent of Divine Intervention to mitigate their effects—but still they occur; the whole world is in a ferment of change, in which many old and much-loved forms are being swept away. But the forecasts of inundations and destruction on a continental scale are based on nothing more than fear—a fear stimulated and maintained by the forces of evil, in their "backs-to-the-wall" fight against their inevitable defeat—and a misunderstanding of time-focus.

The continental shifts and destruction of land masses to which most of the prognostications refer, are not due to occur until some 800 years from now. By that time a more mentally polarised humanity, with the aid of the then externalised Hierarchy, will find themselves well able to cope. All proceeds under law. This misunderstanding of Revelations and Nostradamus is leading to an unhealthy over-emphasis on disaster—thus engendering fear—which I, for one, am doing my best to correct. This is a time of the utmost *hope* and *promise* for mankind.

Violence Today

5/3/76

Is the violence in the world today—in Africa and Ireland and places like that—the final expression of the violence of the world wars, or is it something else, and will it be worked out?

It will inevitably be worked out, but the causes are various.

It seems to be coming up very much . . . in particular in Africa.

Yes, there are several factors here. Much of the violence today is really the result of man's non-realisation of his true nature, of the fact that he is really, fundamentally, a soul—a soul in incarnation; that this personality is a vehicle for a great entity, the soul. The violence in the world today is the result of the imbalance between his inner knowledge of himself as a soul, and his inability to manifest this on the outer plane—through conditioning by society, the lack of education to this effect, and by the point in evolution which the majority of humanity has reached. This produces a situation where man is at war with himself and therefore with the society of which he is a part. A great deal of the violence in the world has this as a cause.

Much of the violence in Africa and elsewhere is the result of emerging peoples searching for, and fighting for, nationhood; throwing off the yoke of Colonialism. The different factions within these developing peoples naturally, given existing economic conditions, seek to impose their own solution and ideology; aided and abetted, of course, by one or other of the major powers, who seek a field of influence for themselves. The only solution to all of this violent struggle is *sharing*.

The Reappearance and Government

I'd like to ask about the Masters of the Wisdom working in co-operation with the governments. The change doesn't have to come about from simply working through existing structures. It can come about through simply withdrawing from those structures.

What is necessary is a total change in our social structure throughout the world. This involves, in the first place, working through the existing governmental structures in order to change them. The involvement of all sections of society in the construction of the new order will ensure the speedy adoption of the necessary measures, so that in this process, the very nature of government, as we visualise it today, will change. It is an incorrect assumption on your part that I see a perpetuation of the existing forms of government; personally I do not at all.

New forms of government might grow up without any actual conflict with the old ones. It's like a cartoon I saw with a priest standing in the church, and the church is completely empty. And he is saying "I am gathered here . . ." There hasn't been any actual conflict, everyone has simply withdrawn from this structure, and left the leader without anyone to lead.

But there are situations in which the leader does in fact lead, and those who are led are also participants in the measures. I am not in any sense envisaging an authoritarian form of government. Not at all. That is entirely out of line with the requirements for the full participation by all sections of society, and the right kind of relationship which must be evolved among free men.

I was questioning all government. In other words, I wasn't making any distinction between democratic, on the one hand, and authoritarian on the other.

Yes, but no matter what form of organisation that we use to live out our social life, it must be through some form of government—whether that government sits in a special place we call Westminster or the Kremlin, or wherever; or whether it is through workshops, or through community gatherings. Government is organisation of relationships. There must be some structure or organisation where decisions are taken for certain results to pertain. That is government; whether it is on a community level, a personal level, or an international level, it would still have some formal structure. What I am suggesting is that the governmental system will change by the participation of *all* sections of society in this process of change. What we today call the democratic system, or the communistic system, or the fascistic system—are all in process of transition towards something else. They are all in a more or less transitory stage, and no one at this moment can foresee exactly the form of government which will pertain in any given country in ten years' time. What I am talking about will begin to take place over the next few years. It is something very immediate, and we shall see, in this country, in the next few years, great changes in our social structure.

7/2/78

Does this imply some sort of world government, what you have outlined?

Inevitably, this will *lead* to world government. World government will not be imposed on mankind but will be the result of the manifested brotherhood. The sharing and the co-operation of all mankind, the redistribution of the produce of the world, will result in world government. Any attempt to achieve or impose world government without the acceptance of sharing is doomed to failure.

7/2/78

What position would the Christ occupy in such a world government?

In the world government itself, as I understand it at this moment—I am not speaking from absolute knowledge—but as I understand it, not in the government at all. At the head of several of the governments of the world and in the great world agencies, like United Nations agencies, and so on, there will be either a Master or at least a third degree Initiate. So the great international agencies will be under the direct control of a high member of the Hierarchy. The Christ will be, not distant from humanity, but the leader. He will show the way, outline the possibilities, outline the Plan. He will be the World Teacher. The Masters will gradually be coming in with Their high Initiates and will oversee the administrative and technical detailed work. The Christ Himself will have a great deal to do—with the release of energies; the work of Initiation, as the Initiator, the Hierophant, at the first two Initiations; and in stimulating and inspiring the formation of the New World Religion.

169

26/7/77

Will there eventually be a world language?

The international language of the future will be English. A simplified English. That is not to say that every nationality will not keep its own language. It will, but there will be an international language of a basic English.

7/2/78

The United Nations must surely be coming under the focus more and more of the Hierarchy—because they've been rather ineffective for a long time—if they are going to become a custodian of resources?

Yes. The energy of the Avatar of Synthesis actually plays through the United Nations Assembly and is slowly but surely bringing the nations together. It is one of the major groupings through which that energy flows. We see the limitations of the United Nations, but the United Nations' Agencies are doing tremendous work all over the world; have been doing, since their inauguration, in all fields—the economic, the ecological, the medical, and the social field—tremendous work of reconstruction and reorganisation. One shouldn't underestimate that contribution to world need which the nations, jointly, are making. This sense of caring is altogether new in world affairs, and a sure indication that the Plan is working out.

7/2/78

What sort of sacrifices are we here going to be called upon to make?

Well, we shall be called upon to live a great deal more simply than we are living now. Mankind—I am not talking about the underdeveloped two-thirds of the world—will enter what is called the "wilderness experience". It will have to learn to live more simply; to learn to share, and all that sharing means; to look on all the produce of the world as belonging to the world as a whole—not American wheat, or Russian oil, or British manufactures, or whatever—but that every nation has assets and these belong to all men, to all nations. Each nation will be asked to draw up an inventory of all that it possesses and all that it needs and this will be made over to the United Nations. All goods and all produce will have to be made over. I say "have to"; it is up to us to endorse this. Nothing will be forced on us. But the advice of Hierarchy and the Christ will be to do this—to make over, in trust for all men, the produce of the world—to be held by United Nations agencies in trust for all, so that no country owns anything. Then that will be distributed among all mankind according to need. This will mean for the developed third of the world an entirely new and simpler living which will be seen to be a great deal happier, for there is nothing easier to bear than something shared. I mean, if you haven't very much, it is easier if no one else has very much.

This is a relative thing. I am not saying we are going to be living in abject poverty, not at all. There is a surplus of food in the world. There is a surplus of raw materials and energy sources, if correctly used.

The Masters have custodianship of scientific knowledge of which we don't even dream at the moment. They have the knowledge of means of power, nuclear power, simple and safe, which would answer the energy demands of all mankind. That is the crux of the situation today. It is all to do with energy. Whoever has the energy today has the power. That energy and therefore that power will be shared by all mankind.

28/3/78

A lot of countries today want to practice deomcracy. How will they take to a Hierarchy?

I have found, especially among the young and politically attuned, democratically oriented, young people today, a great resistance to the idea of Hierarchy. There is quite a resistance to the idea of the Masters of the Wisdom because of the word Hierarchy. Even to the word "Master". Of course the word Master, and the word Hierarchy, do not denote any kind of authority, and what the young today resent very much is authority. They are born into the world with the ideas of freedom, equality, and brotherhood. This is right, this is what

Hierarchy teaches, and this is what the Christ will teach. But Hierarchy is a fact in nature. It is perfectly possible to believe in, and demonstrate your belief in, equality, brotherhood, and liberty, and at the same time to recognise yourself and all others as being at some point on a ladder of evolution. We are all equal under God. But taking part in a long and apparently endless evolutionary journey, we are all of us at some point on that journey. Some are ahead and some have still very far to go. The Masters have completed the journey. They are at the top of the ladder. They stand at the top and They bend down and hold Their hand out to give the next one a hoist up. And he puts his hand down and gives the one below him a hoist up. And so on, down and down the ladder until you get to the least evolved. From the most primitive members of the human race to the Christ, and beyond, is a hierarchy. There are always those who are more evolved, more advanced—they are not better, they are simply more advanced on the evolutionary path. They are demonstrating more of their potential, which is divine.

As souls we are all One. On the soul plane there is no such thing really as an individual soul. There is only an individual aspect of one great Oversoul. As that soul incarnates, involves itself in matter, it has started a journey of return to that perfection from which it came. The soul is perfect. It is a reflection of a perfection, a reflection of the Spirit, the spark of God. We on this physical plane are a reflection of our soul. We are really threefold beings. As that soul incarnates, begins its evolutionary journey, it sets in motion a whole series of events. These make up our successive lives, down through the ages. Over and over again, we incarnate and reincarnate, in group formation, and gradually evolve, gradually demonstrate more and more of our true human—which is also divine—nature. Until we become perfect, like the Masters are perfect. Then we stand at the top of the ladder and we are free to go on to the higher worlds, or we can stay behind and help the one below. The Masters Who have stayed behind on the earth are doing this. It is a part of Their service.

Souls have come into incarnation at different times. The

Masters of the Wisdom are where They are because They began before us. The advanced units of humanity today are where they are in relation to others because they began before them. There is inevitably a hierarchy.

There is hierarchy in the solar system. The planets themselves are at different stages of evolution. Hierarchy is everywhere in cosmos. There is nothing else, in a sense, but hierarchy. At the same time there is no hierarchy because there is no separation. All is one. It is only in manifestation that hierarchy occurs. Out of manifestation, all *is* one. In relation to the whole, each one is a part of the whole, and an equal part of the whole.

The acorn has all the potential of the whole tree within it, and every little seedling is equal, but there are great oaks and little oaks. Those who are more advanced, being more advanced, have both the right and the responsibility to serve more. They have the potential to serve more. This is what advancement is about.

When that Hierarchy is seen to be of a genuinely Spiritual nature, people will find that it is not impossible to construct a truly democratic form of government (there is no true democracy today) which, at the same time, partakes somewhat of the Hierarchical mode of relationship.

When men realise the need for guidance on the path of life which leads to perfection, and when man's free-will is not (as it never is by Hierarchy) infringed, they will gladly accept, as normal and right, a degree of Hierarchical guidance based on experience and achievement, which today might appear unlikely.

Work in the Future

6/9/77

As there is so much unemployment in the world, is that an indication that the idea of work will change? I mean, most people work for a living, will that idea change?

Yes. The major area of concern in the immediate future will be

173

the problem of leisure: how mankind will utilise the leisure which he will have. A great many people today, because of the world labour situation, have endless leisure. They don't want it, they don't want to be unemployed, but they have leisure. However, they have not been educated, for the most part, to use that leisure correctly. In this coming time, gradually (I'm not talking about something that is going to happen overnight, but eventually) mankind will create machines which will do the work which today is done by the bulk of humanity. Mankind will be released into a state of leisure which will give him the opportunity to explore his own inner nature, to know what he really is, the great divine Being he really is, and allow him to manifest that quality.

Today, freedom from enforced activity; freedom from want; freedom from hunger; freedom to explore the nature of one's own Being; the freedom to create; is known to a relatively small number of people. It is the privileged few who have this kind of freedom. Most people work to earn enough money to keep themselves and their families, and the vast majority of the people in the world work at deadly, mechanical work which bears no relation to man's true nature, his creativeness. It is not creative work. Some people, of course, enjoy their work immensely, and get a great emotional, mental and spiritual return in terms of energy from that work, because they are deeply engaged in the creative aspects of it. It engages their creativity. But for the vast majority of mankind this is not so.

In the future it will be so. The nature of work will change. We shall have to learn to live much more simply, not geared to this great mechanical civilisation we have built around ourselves, especially in the industrialised West. The Christ and the Masters will show that we can live perfectly happily, even more happily, in a much simpler way, with fewer things. But those things will be beautiful. They will be made because they are needed, and they will be made with the creativeness of man behind them, whether they are man-made or machine-made. A completely new attitude will take place in relation to work. Through the power of sound, man will build and create the

174

artefacts of his civilisation and control his environment, relating it to his real needs.

When he comes into correct relationship to his brother and his Source, he will inherit that Divine Science, which is his birthright, but is known today only by the Masters of the Wisdom.

China and the Plan

21/12/76

There is a very large part of the world where the economic changes you are talking about have already taken place, such as the Peoples Republic of China. Where does this fit into the Plan?

It fits in very much. Whatever of significance happens in any country at all happens under the inspiration of Hierarchy. There is an entire department in the Hierarchy, the Department of the Manu, which deals with the politics of the world: the great movements of the races; the building of races; the forming of nations; the destiny of nations; the working out of the political, governmental and racial divisions of humanity.

Great experiments are going on in China and Russia, America and Great Britain. One of the most interesting today is what is happening in China. It is still very fluid. It is watched with extreme interest by Hierarchy, and could still go in many directions, well, or not so well. The changes which have taken place have had traumatic, chaotic effects in China, for example, the great Cultural Revolution. The kind of changes that I am envisaging, which will take place in the five centres at first, will take place *without* these traumatic effects; in the normal democratic way, by logical legislation and general agreement. All sections of society will take part, which will ensure the adoption of the various changes, whereas in China, and Russia, many of them were imposed. In America and Britain, today, many social changes are opposed by finance rather than by decree, but the result is the same. We don't have democracy today, true democracy. There is no true democracy in the world—not in

175

China, Russia or Britain. We are all moving towards a more perfect expression of the governmental and political systems that we live under.

In the future, the not too distant future, we will come to see that all political systems are divine expressions. There is more in common between *true* Democracy and *true* Communism than there would seem to be today. What is called communism today as it exists in Russia, China and the Communist world, is in no sense true Communism, but it is an evolving structure, moving towards a more perfect expression of the thought-form as it exists in the Divine Mind; likewise with Democracy.

Russia, China and the Prophecies

19/10/76

In the prophecies of Nostradamus, mention is made of war between Russia and China. Does it mean that war will be averted because the Christ is coming now?

If you want my personal opinion, there will be no third world war, either between Russia and China or any other country. Nothing can prevent the Descent of the Christ and the Masters. I would say that Russia has more than enough on its plate to deal with, and China also has many inner problems and tensions, without their going to war with one another. I certainly don't see a war between Russia and China.

But these political systems don't really seem to be working. There is so much conflict. How do you see this being resolved?

Very soon we shall become aware that all political systems, without exception, are in a state of transition, more or less. All of them are changing, all of them are coming to a purer expression of the Hierarchical energy and the Divine intention which is behind them.

All political systems are the result of a Divine thought, a Divine Will, for a certain quality of expression which humanity can give. All of them will shortly be seen to be in this state of transition, and therefore not so mutually exclusive as they now appear to be—and a much greater world harmony will result from this. You will see very shortly the healing of the wounds between the nations. Over this coming year you will see things taking place which you would not have thought possible. There will be greater *détente*, greater synthesis.

There is standing behind the Christ a great Avatar, called the Avatar of Synthesis, and it was His energy, largely, that we transmitted at the beginning of the meeting. He is a great Cosmic Entity. His energy is a fourfold expression: all the energies or aspects of God we know about—Will, Love and Intelligence, plus another quality for which we don't even have a name yet. We don't even recognise this quality yet. This fourfold synthetic energy is pouring into the world, through the Christ, then through the groups and disciples of the world, bringing them together. It works only through groups; through the United Nations Assembly, through Hierarchy, through humanity as a group, and above all through the New Group of World Servers; and it is bringing humanity together, making humanity One on the physical plane, which it already is on the inner plane.

Another great entity standing behind the Christ is the Spirit of Peace or Equilibrium. He is overshadowing the Christ, in a very similar way to the way the Christ overshadowed and worked through the disciple Jesus in Palestine. He works very closely with the law of Action and Reaction, and His function is to transform the prevalent discord, confusion, chaos, turmoil in the world into its opposite, so that we shall enter an era of tranquillity and peace—in exact proportion to the present discord. The violence and hatred of today will be transmuted into goodwill, and again, in exact proportion to the intensity of the hatred and violence. This is the great Law of Action and Reaction functioning. The law stated is that action and reaction are equal and opposite, and this great Cosmic Entity, the Spirit of Equilibrium, is working now through the Christ, producing the transformation of the world.

27/1/76

Russia and China—do you foresee a clash in the future?

The short answer to that is "No". Russia has, fundamentally, the good of humanity at heart; has at the basis of its approach to life, the idea that men are brothers. This is true despite the harsh and cruel imposition of a system where there is a lack of free speech, movement and belief. Despite that, fundamental to the Soviet people, is this belief that men are One, that humanity is One. And basically, in the Chinese revolution, is the same idea. There is no reason in their respective political ideology to go to war. What the tension is really about is an attempt to claim the adherence, for their particular brand of communism, of the Third World. They are fighting politically and ideologically for that. Very soon, the nations of the world will realise that all political systems have much in common.

There is a similarity of intention in America, Russia and Britain for instance (Britain representing the Commonwealth of Nations; Britain in Europe represents a larger body of thinking along the same lines). They are not identical but there is a wide common ground and that common ground will find its expression in the transition of each of their political systems into something which won't be identical—there is no reason at all why each nation should have exactly the same political system—but they will grow into a kind of relationship which makes co-existence not only possible but natural and inevitable. The acceptance of the principle of *sharing* will make this inevitable.

28/2/79

At present there is war between Vietnam and China; don't you think this is just the beginning of those wars prophesied about by many seers in the past?

As I understand it, the Hierarchical attitude to this is that it will not develop into that prophesied war between Russia and China.

What mediums, seers and those making predictions do,

bringing in information, usually from the astral plane, is take up a thought-form. There is a potent thought-form about destruction. This comes primarily from the reading of Revelations (in the Bible), Nostradamus, and various other prognostications, which have existed for hundreds of years, and in the case of Revelations nearly 2,000 years. Thought-forms of catastrophe and destruction at the end of the age have been created in men's minds.

There are two kinds of thought-forms: those which are mental and those which are the result of man's fears—these are unreal. But they become real, because every thought is real. Even if it is an astral thought-form, it is still a potent force although it has no essential reality. What is happening at present is that the forces of evil are fighting a last-ditch stand, because they know that with the Christ and the Hierarchy in the world they are doomed. They are going to be sealed off to their own domain for 3,000 years, and they will not be able to affect mankind in the same way. Hence their present desperate fight to foment, as potently as they can, this fear reflex in mankind. They work through fear. They work mostly on the physical and astral planes, but also on the lower mental planes. They create fear, anxiety and chaos.

They are doing this by focusing their attention on and stimulating these thought-forms of destruction and catastrophe, so that they should become a reality. If mankind surrounds himself with a thought-form potently enough, sooner or later he creates a situation in which that thought-form works out. That is how our actions work out. We create our own life from moment to moment, through creating thought-forms. Thought-forms are active, potent forces and they rebound on us, for good or ill. We are all the the time creating living processes, which may be positive or negative. The idea of catastrophe has become very potent on the astral plane, and is utilised by the forces of evil in this way. In response to this, certain actions are carried out on the physical plane which in fact bring about that which is feared, as a reflex.

All I can say at present is that Hierarchy is not worried about the situation in China. Obviously, They would prefer that it

179

had not taken place. But there is such a thing as the partial embodiment of a thought-form. By letting the thought-form work out partially, the greater sting of the total embodiment of the thought-form is taken away. For instance, many disciples may be due at a certain moment to suffer some illness or accident by karmic law. If their karmic situation and their relationship to their Master permit, that Master can intervene, and draw the sting or venom out of the happening. The person will be ill or have a slight accident, but it won't be as bad as it might have been, if there had been the full karmic result. Now it may be that what we are witnessing in China today is of such a nature.

It may be that the venom from the fangs of the forces of evil is being drawn off by the Hierarchy, and by the fact of the Christ in the world, and in this way allow it to work out rather more mildly than might otherwise have been the case. This is the transmutation process which Hierarchy always uses. It is the way They fight the forces of evil. So They are not at this moment worried.

Karl Marx

14/12/78

You mentioned that Marx was working for the Hierarchy, which surprises me, I would have thought that he was working for the Dark Forces.

Marx was indeed a member of the Hierarchy, of a certain degree. Looking at the effect of his work over the years—that could only have been the work of a disciple of some degree, an initiate of some level: first, to have the vision, and secondly, to have the capacity to embody that vision so that the work could spread.

He came into the world to release a certain teaching about new economic possibilities, new relationships, a new theory of social change, and he built it into a very structured dialectic. You can accept it or reject it. Many countries are using Marxism as a basis, but are producing very different forms of communistic theory. One can interpret it, and use it as one wishes, according to what is needed. It is a tool for the understanding of the historical process along political-economic lines.

Marxism is feared today, in some countries, because it means change—that's what it's about; he is the apostle of change, of perpetual changes, even changes within Marxism. Of course, at present, if a smaller "Marxist" country advocates change within the Marxist structure, the bigger powers step in and prevent it, as happened with Czechoslovakia and Russia. They know that this is infectious, and could and would lead to similar revolution in Russia. That would mean the overthrow of the oligarchy which imposes a rather mechanical interpretation of Marxism on its people.

Marxism is not only a narrow economic theory, it is to do with the basic laws of mankind's nature and inter-relationship. Man is One. That, essentially, is what Marx is saying. Man is One, Humanity is One. Eventually, all social systems will tend towards a system which encourages that brotherhood or Oneness of man which Marx senses, as a spiritual Being. His vision is a spiritual one, but has been taken up by lesser men, who have imposed the theory. The fault is in the *imposition* of the theory, for the satisfaction of their own ambition for power.

Of course, he had his limitations—every disciple has. Dialectical materialism is an oversimplification of man's many-sided reality, but was needed to focus his thinking along new political/economic lines. Marx's main weakness was that in sweeping away glamours and superstitions, especially in the great peasant countries of the world, he also swept away the concept of God. That is the Church's quarrel with Marxism: He emphasised man's Oneness in economic terms, not in religious terms.

The Women's Movement

14/1/77

I find it interesting that there has been a definite raising of conscious-

181

ness in women in the last few years. The women's movement has really got under way. It has developed in a big way. And women are changing tremendously. Also women tend to be more sensitive than men. They always have been, you know, they have more intuition and so on. And logically it seems to me that it is quite possible the Christ could come in a female body.

It might seem to follow. Womankind through the ages has not accepted totally its energetic role—which is the fault of women and the fault of humanity in general. What is needed is a balance of the male and female energies on the physical plane through the release of the female potential you mentioned. The female role is the nourishing of civilisation. This is behind the whole female principle. The female, the mother, representing the matter aspect, is the nourisher of the planet, the nourisher of mankind, and all the kingdoms in nature. The male aspect brings in the creative stimulating energy. The result of the fusion of the two is the Christ, which is Man, or the Christ Principle. This principle the female aspect nourishes. To do this properly, women have to come into their own, they have to release their full potential as human beings, and so make a balance between the matter aspect and the spirit aspect on this planet—I'm talking in terms of energy—and when this takes place, you will have Masters in female bodies. For the present, all Masters, including the Christ, are in male bodies.

5/3/76

Will women's liberation recognise the Christ when He manifests?

No doubt, some of them will. Women's liberation is a manifestation of a very specific and serious Hierarchical intention. It is absolutely necessary that humanity realises that the male and female are in polarity. Energetically, both are necessary on the planet—not the domination of one by the other. The Women's Liberation movement is Hierarchically inspired. It is, at the moment, slightly off-key, due to being led at present by women who have a somewhat neurotic hatred of men, forgetting that they themselves have been men over and over again, throughout their incarnational experience. And so, perhaps understandably, they blame men entirely for their difficulties and their lack of freedom. But the lack of freedom of women in the world is real—very real indeed, and must give way to full equal rights.

Effect on Family Life

28/3/78
Do you see the break-up of the nuclear family and more communal living?

More communal living, yes. The family is the basic unit of humanity. The baby is cradled in the family, and the mother is the nourisher. She nourishes the baby and looks after it, sees it comes to no harm and teaches it—imparts whatever level of civilisation she has to the child.

The family, as far as humanity is concerned, is the basic building brick and cannot be dispensed with. I know there are many experiments going on—in the kibbutzim and various communities—to dispense with the family as a unit, and they are having various degrees of success for certain lengths of time. However, in many of them they are finding that no matter how hard they try, when the children who are born and brought up in such a situation reach maturity, again and again they return to the family unit. It would seem to be a basic, essential part of man's nature, and certainly it is crucial in the progress of the race, of the evolving sons of men, as they come into incarnation, because the family provides the form for the incoming ego.

The aim is that egos of higher and higher and more expanded consciousness can come in to serve the race, but they can only come in if the bodies are provided. It is only in bodies of the right quality, right vibrational rate, the right relationship provided by the family that they can come in.

So the family is essential, We choose our families. We don't choose a group; we are part of a group. We incarnate as groups and choose the father and the mother, which is our family, who

183

will provide the body which our soul, our true self, sees will give the approximation in vibrational rate, and opportunity therefore, to the kind of level which we as souls are evidencing, at any given point, as we incarnate.

The family unit will be retained, but it will be seen to be possible to hold the family unit within a wider group and community relationship. It will not be the break-up of the family, but the extension of family units.

Take for example, a triangle. If you break up a triangle, you lose the force of the triangle. A triangle is a highly potent force unit—much more potent than the three separate parts which make it up. When you join up these triangles at their points, you get a tremendously powerful field of interlocked energies. That is like the family, the nuclear family, in the relationship of the groups. When you break up the family, there is a loss of Egoic intention. The nourishing aspect goes. The mother is the nourisher, and nourishes the civilisation, just as those nations which are feminine nourish the civilisation. The role of the woman is to nourish, so that particular family aspect has to be kept, but expanded to include a wider expression of itself, without losing its essential energetic role.

So the isolation of the nuclear family will cease?

The isolation of the nuclear family is an artificial thing, brought about by our divided civilisation today. Where co-operation exists between men and the growth of communities comes about, then automatically you get a growth of interrelated family units, which remain family units. Then will come the growth of groups and communities until the whole of humanity is one group, one community, as it essentially is.

17/2/77

What about the break-down of family life?

Everything is breaking down. All the old institutions—and the family is also one of the institutions—are breaking down. Everyone is under tremendous strain and stress. Families are to do with relationship. The new time is to do with the restructuring of our relationships; the extending of our allegiance and our identification from the family to a larger group, from the larger group to the community, from the community to the community of nations. It is always a greater and greater expansion of identification. It is relatively easy to love one's family, well, easier to love one's family than to love the world!

There are many people together as families who shouldn't be together. In order to really make a proper marriage there should be a similarity of vibration, of ray quality, and some identity on the physical, emotional, mental and the spiritual realms. These are four levels on which people should equate in a perfect marriage. You get people who are physically attracted but mentally and emotionally are not compatible with each other. In other instances, you might get people who are completely compatible on the soul level, on the mental level, even on the emotional level, but who are physically incompatible. So it is very difficult. In the future our partners will be chosen in a much more scientific way, according to Ray quality, karmic relationship, and point in evolution. The family break-down is a temporary factor due to the wider break-down of our social structures, and our limited knowledge of ourselves.

28/3/78

If the Christ is bringing in a different love aspect—I don't want to be facetious—but the love between husband and wife and family, will that be altered in any way, if they have to include love to everybody else?

The Christ does not bring in a *different* love aspect. He brings the love aspect in a more potent form than ever before because He is overshadowed now by the Spirit of Peace or Equilibrium, Who is transmitting love from a very high cosmic level through Him into the world. This makes it possible for Him to Embody the Christ Consciousness in an even more potent way than before. It doesn't alter it.

It is easier for husband and wife, and parents and children to

185

stand in a love relationship than to stand in a love relationship with people one doesn't know, with people in other nations, with whom one's own country may have been at war, or something like that. But the Christ has brought the energy of love in such intensity, such potency today, that mankind will be enabled to include relationships into its love nature which up to now has been very difficult.

It is relatively very difficult for nations to love one another. The nation is the expression of the qualities and development of the individuals in the nation. Just as individuals, governed by energies called Rays, are all on different Rays, so nations are also governed by different Rays. Some nations find it comparatively easy to see the other's point of view; they seem to think alike; they have things in common.

Other nations find it very difficult. They don't seem to have qualities or ways of thinking in common. This is entirely dependent on the Ray qualities governing the nations. As the energy of Love makes itself felt more and more, through the action of the Christ, we shall be able to expand our ability to love in the true sense—I mean love in the inclusive, not the emotional sense—to embrace our community and our nation and our international community.

Most men, or a lot of men, have what we call patriotism, love of country. Many are—they have shown this—ready to die for their country. But to expand that, to die for other countries, is a different kind of love (I am not talking about mercenaries who also die for other countries; they die for the money). To include all mankind in one's love is a very difficult thing indeed and requires, and is evidence of, a relatively high level of development. Gradually, as the work and the teaching of the Christ grows in this coming age, mankind will develop this kind of inclusive love. It may still be only on the emotional level, but gradually they will begin to manifest love in the sense that the Masters know it—as a totally impersonal, inclusive, magnetic force. The Masters call it Pure Reason and there is no emotion in it at all. It is something which today only very advanced individuals can express.

What mankind has expressed in the last 2,000 years is the

energy of knowledge. Our science and our educational systems are the expression of this. In the next 2,000 years we shall express the love of God, not only the intelligence of God. The Christ will bring a yet higher aspect than Love, the Will aspect, but of course it will only become manifest in individuals. In the following cycle, or towards the end of this cycle, more and more of humanity will begin to evidence that quality of Will which includes Love.

President Sadat/President Carter

19/1/78

The Christ was obviously behind the change of heart between Egypt and Israel?

He was indeed behind the change of heart between Egypt and Israel. President Sadat reacted to the direct impress of the Mind of the Christ. This is what is meant when the Christ said recently, Message No. 9 given on November 3rd 1977: "Many there are who doubt My Presence. This is natural. Men are blind. But soon there will be no gainsaying. My efforts will show men that the wheel turns, that soon the New Time, the New World, will have commenced. May it be that you will share in this work." And the *rapprochement*, that unheard of thing, that unbelievable *rapprochement* between Egypt and Israel is the direct result of that. Those of you who have been attending these meetings regularly will know that in December 1976 I forecast that this would take place, and within a year. Nothing is fixed yet, of course. The Middle East is still one of the central problems facing mankind.

The *primary* problem facing mankind is the distribution of the food and with it the raw materials and the energy resources of the world. That is the fundamental, the primary human problem—to share the food and so save the starving millions. Then, politically, the next problem is to resolve the situation in the Middle East, solve the Arab-Israeli problem. It is a powder-keg which could (and did, several times) erupt into

187

war, and could have erupted into a world war by drawing the great nations in on one side or the other. So it is interesting, and to me not surprising, that that was the first major political action resulting from the efforts of the Christ since coming in, on July 19th last year (1977).

26/4/77

On what level is Jimmy Carter? He seems to fit in with the level of programme of activities of which you have spoken?

He is a remarkable man and is reacting to the stimulus of the Hierarchy. Much will come out of the actions of that man. It is not so much what he initiates as that he will be open to certain suggestions put forward by younger men, trained by the Masters. He himself is a highly evolved being, open to impression by Hierarchy; consciously a man of spiritual intent, with a great altruism. His coming into power in America at this present moment is, of course, no accident.

You will see more and more younger men coming into positions of influence and power in all the major governments of the world. This is part of the Plan for the reappearance of the Christ. They will be more sensitive and more responsive to the newer ideas.

Young People Today

26/4/77

You say that the governments will have to be led by younger people. Now it does strike a lot of my sort of generation, not because we want to hog the scene, but it does seem often—our experience of living has led us on to a path that does seem very different from a lot of the young people who are very badly at sea spiritually. And it intrigues me—there must be, evidently, some young people who are not like that?

In my opinion it is precisely young people today who have the new spiritual vision; who see the world as One; who believe in love and brotherhood and sharing; who are ready to share. It is

188

easy to say: "I agree with the Christ. I am all for sharing the produce", but in fact, what does it mean? It means that we in the developed West who greedily grab and waste most of the food, energy and raw materials of the world, have got to learn to live more simply. The rest of the world, two-thirds of it, live at the lowest level.

We have to be sure in ourselves whether we are ready for this experience; whether we are ready to relinquish what we have in surplus in order to share what we have with all. Are we ready for this sharing? That is what we have to ask ourselves. It won't be done for us. We have to see within ourselves if we are ready. The hearts of mankind, according to Hierarchy, are sound. These qualities of sharing and co-operation are deeply imbedded in the hearts of millions of people, especially in the young; above all in the young.

It is the young who will inherit this coming time. They have come into incarnation specifically. Every generation brings into incarnation those who can deal with the problems which they will meet. This is the law. We come into incarnation in group formation, specially equipped to deal with the situations. This is what is happening now. The young are equipped, mentally and spiritually, to deal with the problems which beset us today.

When I say younger men—the average age of politicians today is probably about 65—I mean much younger men. I don't mean teenagers, but I mean much younger men. President Carter is only 54, which is a young man, by these standards. Others are much younger still.

World Resources

24/9/76

By whom are all the resources of the world given to all mankind?

By that Being Whose body of manifestation the planet is—the Logos of our planet. When the food, raw materials, and energy sources are flowing steadily, equally distributed throughout all mankind, the result is health. When any of it is dammed up at

189

any point you get stasis, you get inflammation and disease. That is the root cause of the malaise of the world—the fact that one-third of the planet usurps and wastes most of the food, raw materials, and energy resources, while two-thirds go without. That imbalance is creating a diseased world. Hence the tension and violence.

Every healer knows that disease in man occurs when there is a disturbance, a dis-equilibrium, in our etheric envelope or subtle-body. The free flow of that energy is interrupted at some point or points, stasis or inflammation occur, and eventuate on the dense physical level as disease of some kind or other. So it is in the body of the planet as a whole. Right flow and right distribution of nature's resources is essential for planetary health and well-being. War is a result of failure to observe this Law.

19/7/77

Famine is not really famine is it, because the food exists?

The food exists. It is simply not distributed. The Hierarchy have plans already made, ready to be put into effect when the will is there, which will equally distribute the food. There is a group of high Initiates—industrialists, economists, administrators, of great experience and achievement—who, with Hierarchy, have worked out plans and blueprints which will solve the redistribution problems of the world, when the political will is there to implement them. These plans are there, ready to transform the world. This can be done in no time at all. There is a surplus of food, per capita, of 4 per cent according to U.N. Agencies' statistics. It is not famine. It is the lack of will to implement the process of sharing. It is also the lack of simple, human compassion.

19/3/76

About this premature incarnation of underdeveloped souls—if the world's population is constantly increasing, presumably there will be an even greater number of underdeveloped souls incarnating and therefore violence will be increasing rather than decreasing?

190

That is what is happening now. It is not what will continue to happen. Man will come to realise that the over-population of the world is a grave danger to the continuation of the species. Today, one of the major reasons—and this is the extraordinary paradox—for the huge population in the world, is the over-population of the poorer areas of the world, the Third World, those nations least able to afford to feed their peoples. In the modern, advanced, rich, well-nourished Western European and American nations, you have a relatively low population growth rate. But in the Third World, you have huge families, seven, eight, nine and more in a family, for one reason only: they are dependent on having large families because they know that two-thirds or more will die before they can grow up; and the traditional peasant outlook on families as people to look after them in their old age. That is their insurance, their pension for the future, because they don't have pensions. They have large families in many areas of the world simply to ensure that one, two, or maybe three will live into adulthood. The rest will surely die because the food of the world is not distributed among the needy of the world. If this food were distributed, distributed tomorrow; if the energy sources, the technical know-how, were shared throughout the world, no one would feel the necessity of having large families to ensure that they were supported in their old age.

These are the facts of the case. The answer also is plain. When we take these steps; when we share the produce of the world, you will see that the masses of poor people who are producing most of the forms for the incarnating egos will take the steps needed to prevent this, and gradually the population will subside to a level which the planet can easily bear.

30/8/77

How soon will there be a time when we shan't need to have food, as we do today?

Thinking ahead, the more advanced members of the race will live directly off prana from the sun. But that is a long way ahead for most of us. I know I, for one, am not ready for that!

191

24/1/78

How will the return of the Christ affect the way we live, materially?

We shall enter a much simpler mode of life. The Christ will show that we have to live more simply in order that all men may live. Having done that, with the science of which the Hierarchy are the custodians, we can in a relatively short time enter a period of bountiful material plenty, because by then we will have learned how to live according to the Law—the Laws which are God. When we live within the Law, which is the Will of God, we are allowed the knowledge, we are able to handle the knowledge, which will enable us to live in material plenty—*but putting materiality in its place*. Today we are totally shackled by materialism. The world today wants more and more of everything—growth in all systems is the aim. Every nation wants more and more growth. We shall have to learn to live more simply, which means entering, from the industrial point of view, what has been called a steady-state economy, so that we produce only what we need. By keeping production to that relative need, growth in industry becomes a thing of the past. But with the new science which the Masters will show us how to use, we shall be able to manufacture machinery which will take from man the need to work mechanically and so free him for true creativity.

Vegetarianism

22/6/76

Is vegetarianism the proper diet for the Aquarian Age?

The Aquarian Age will be the age of right relationship, the age of reason, the age of brotherhood and love. This right relationship, of which reason, brotherhood and love are the expression, will be right relationship between all the kingdoms: between Man and his Source, which is Reality or God, however you envisage God; between man and man; and between man and the animal, vegetable and mineral kingdoms.

192

All the kingdoms will come into a very active, dynamic relationship as humanity comes, more and more, into a conscious relationship with the next kingdom, above the human—the Spiritual Kingdom or the Kingdom of Souls, which is made up of the Masters and Initiates in the Hierarchy. Through the teaching of the Masters and through the grounding in the human consciousness of the Plan which issues from Shamballa, mankind will come to realise his true destiny, which is to act as a great clearing-house for energies flowing through him to the lower kingdoms. So he will see that he has a great responsibility, on the planet, to the other kingdoms in Nature, and a change in his relationship to the animal kingdom will take place.

Inevitably, out of this change will come, generally, a vegetarian diet for mankind. This will be the norm. That is not to say that the eating of meat today by large masses of mankind is wrong. There is no single group diet today—one diet for all men. There are groups in the world today where the eating of meat is not only normal and right but essential: for instance, how else could the Eskimo live? Is he going to everlasting hell-fire because he eats meat? In time, when the true relationship between man and the lower kingdoms is seen, a more sane and balanced approach to diet will come about.

Vegetarianism becomes the norm, becomes essential (but I don't mean to make that "essential" an imperative) for the man who seeks to take Initiation; who is making a conscious effort to advance along the evolutionary path; who is taking a hand in his own evolution. At some point along that evolutionary path vegetarianism does become necessary. Not simply because it is "wrong" to kill animals, but because the vibrational rate of the animal body, in particular the blood of the animal, is inimical to the higher vibrational rate which he is seeking to establish in his centres. He is seeking to attract to himself atomic particles of higher and higher vibration. This is what evolutionary or spiritual advancement is—vibrating to a higher and higher frequency. The eating of meat may be perfectly normal and right for average man, but for the aspirant, and the disciple on the Path to Initiation, the eating of meat is detrimental, in that it lowers his vibrational rate.

Common sense is the great thing in all this. You eat what you find through a minimum requirement keeps your body healthy. Each individual and each group finds for itself the diet which suits its purposes, climate, tradition and background. That is for today. But in the New Age vegetarianism will become the norm.

22/3/77

If we had evolved more perfectly should we be using electricity rather than oil?

We live in an electrical universe. There isn't anything else in the whole of the universe but electricity. We know of, and touch, the lowest aspect of that. One of the great secrets which will be released into the world when the Mystery Schools are open and the age-old Mysteries are revealed, in this coming time, is the secret of electricity in its higher aspects. That holds the key to the power of the universe, and some of that power will be released to man under the guidance of Hierarchy, when we are ready. It is one of the Revelations. It is right that we use it, yes, indeed, because we are touching God.

The energy forms of today—coal, gas, oil and electricity in its lower aspect—are all interim measures until we have, under the inspiration of Hierarchy, the higher electrical forces, released in the first place from the atoms of water.

Nuclear Energy—Now and in the Future

22/3/77

What will happen to all the nuclear weapons that exist in the world now after the emergence of the Hierarchy?

They will be neutralised. It is a simple thing to neutralise the negative nuclear force in the bombs; or which is prevalent in

194

our drinking water, in the atmosphere, and so on. There is a simple science which neutralises the effect of negative nuclear activity.

6/9/77

There's a danger of an atomic war—annihilation by accident— now. Do you think the coming of the Master can prevent that?

The coming of the Christ can make—I won't say makes sure—but can make as sure as makes no difference, the unlikelihood of the nations throwing themselves at each others throats, using atomic weapons. One of the reasons why He comes now is to act as the Agent of Divine Intervention; and He comes now, in particular, "like a thief in the night" as He said He would come, way ahead of expectation; when the world doesn't seem ready, to many people, for the appearance of the Christ. He has come to make sure that that possibility does not arise. If an atomic war happened today, or at any time in the future, for the first time in history the Lord of the World Himself, Sanat Kumara, would be directly involved. This has never been the case. Sanat Kumara, the Lord of the World, on Shamballa, gave permission for the release of the atomic secrets to the Allies during the war. This was released through the fifth and seventh Ray Ashrams in the Hierarchy to the scientists working on the Allied side. They were able to manufacture and perfect the atomic bomb ahead of the Axis Powers.

If that had been otherwise—and there was a period of four months in 1942 when both these forces were running neck and neck for this secret—this could have resulted in the Axis Powers gaining the secret first and threatening the annihilation of mankind. This would have led us into a great new dark age. It would have put back the evolution of this planet for millennia. That was prevented by the intervention of the Lord of the World Himself, so He would now be directly involved in any use of atomic weapons. So every step will be taken to prevent such a thing. But, of course, mankind has free-will.

Could you say something about the role, if any, of nuclear energy in the new age?

There is a role for nuclear energy, but not the type of nuclear energy we are using today, through the fission process. That is highly dangerous. The *fusion* process is the method for the immediate future, and that is, as you know, being explored in this country, in the United States, and elsewhere. It will use a form of nuclear energy derived from a single isotope of water. It is safe, and superabundant in the waters of the oceans and rivers of the world. This nuclear fusion uses not heat, but a cold process, and will be used relatively very soon, not immediately, but in the coming five to ten years. (Our own scientists estimate the perfecting of this process to take fifteen to twenty years, but this will be tremendously speeded up by the presence of the Hierarchy, openly, in the world.)

This will supply all the energy needs of the planet—for every village, every town, every city throughout the world. Can you imagine the result? It will release mankind from using other forms of energy (of which some nations have more and some less) and free man from drudgery.

There is a more advanced form than the fusion process. This is part of the Divine Science which will eventually be ours, revealed by the Masters. This entails the release, through the power of mind, of the energy inherent in the etheric counterpart of crystals. In this way we shall come to use directly, and safely, the energy of the etheric ocean in which we live.

Why produce this evil thing which can destroy mankind— plutonium and the use of nuclear energy—and not the use of solar energy which is non-pollutant?

It is a technical problem. There are other ways of using nuclear energy. There is a process now being explored which is a very safe use of the energy inherent in matter. Nuclear energy is the primordial energy after it has become matter. It is released through different processes. It can be released through the fission process which produces plutonium, is highly destructive and deadly, and is that which is used in the atomic bomb. There is also the fusion process, from isotopes of water, plentiful every where in the world. From the fusion process we can have a perfectly safe use of the inherent energy of the universe.

Solar energy is another form; the energy of the tides, which we have barely begun to explore, is another form. These are interim measures. The true energy of the future will be a form of nuclear energy. First of all, as now, through the fission process. Then it will come through fusion, which is basically safe, and all mankind will have any amount of energy. This will release mankind for its true purpose: to explore its true nature. We in the West have had sufficient energy from coal, steam, gas electricity, and nuclear energy for a couple of centuries, but there are large sections of the world which are deeply deficient in energy resources, because they have not the advantage or disadvantage—whichever way you look at it—of our industrial revolution.

The aim is to release mankind for its true destiny; to enable it to explore its own true nature. This means that instead of the bulk of humanity spending nine-tenths of its time as donkeys—that's how the bulk of humanity lives today—abundant energy will free mankind for the creative exploration of his potential. But it will only be possible when *all* of mankind have abundant free energy. This will come through the fusion process.

The discovery of nuclear power was no accident. It was released deliberately to humanity, by Hierarchy. In it lies great benefit. At the moment it is being wrongly used, but in the future it will be used for the greatest benefit of humanity.

This will be the freeing agent for man. In fact, the nuclear age and the age of Maitreya are the same. This, the discovery of the atom, the discovery of atomic power, atomic energy, really is the start of the Aquarian age, symbolically, at least.

Will this automatically affect transport?

Indeed yes, very much so. In this coming time we shall build forms of transport which will be so rapid and so silent that they will seem to be motionless; so apparently motionless and quiet that fatigue will disappear. There will be no vibration; we shall use the natural energies inherent in the atoms of water. Eventually, the most advanced beings will simply *will* themselves here or there, as the Masters do. A Master could appear here now, from wherever He might be. From anywhere in the world He could suddenly come in through that door. It's as simple as that. By an act of will, He could come in His full physical presence.

SOME INDIVIDUALS

Alice A. Bailey

5/3/76

May I ask, having read some of the Alice Bailey books, I wonder—is the information contained therein telepathically received or is it received through a particular line of people who have held the esoteric secrets of the Tibetan Book of the Dead, the Book of Thoth, or is it a burst of sudden illumination which has allowed somebody to set these writings down?

From the Hierarchical point of view, the *Secret Doctrine* of Madame Blavatsky, the founder of the Theosophical Society, represents the preparatory phase of the Teaching given out to the world for this new age. The Teaching embodied in the *Alice Bailey Teachings* represents the intermediate phase of this Teaching. This was given to her by the One Who called Himself for many years simply "the Tibetan", Whom we know now as the Master D.K.—Djwal Khul. Alice Bailey received it by means of the higher telepathy, through the medium of the soul.

If you read her autobiography, you will find that she downright refused to have anything to do with these Teachings and said: "no, I am not going to be a medium", until she was assured by her own Master that this was nothing to do with mediumship, that it was the higher telepathy, that it was work for the Plan, and that it would be in the best interests of the Hierarchy and the world if she would kindly undertake this thirty-year duty—it lasted thirty years. Finally, she agreed and started the work. And so, for thirty years, she was the amanuensis of the Master D.K.

The next stage, the Revelatory Phase, we are told, will emerge, world-wide, through the medium of the radio, after 1975. That is because the Masters and the Christ will soon be in the world, and the Revelations will take place through the medium of the radio (and television).

Edgar Cayce

23/6/77

Can you comment on what Edgar Cayce said? He in fact said that before the end of this century a great new religion would come out of Russia. He also said that the axis of the earth would change. He said that Atlantis would come up. He said that most of the United States would go down and that most of Western Europe would go down too. Also, has the lining up of the planets in 1982 significance—I wonder how you see this?

Yes, the emergence of the new world religion from Russia; I have already spoken about that. It will, the Master D.K. has revealed, emerge from Russia, and it will be a very scientific religion. I don't mean scientific in the sense of some cold, clinical thing, but scientific in the sense of an occult, esoteric religion, dealing with the science of energies, the science of invocation, which will be the keynote of the new religion—invocation will take the place of prayer and worship—and Initiation.

On the raising of Atlantis. Yes, this will take place slowly, is now gradually taking place. Atlantis is slowly rising. It will take about 800 years, though.

What is always very difficult in prophecy (and this is almost as true for the prophecy of the Masters as it is for those like Edgar Cayce who have been the recipients of trance information)—is to place it in a precise time area. The emergence of the new world religion from Russia is said to be this century; that may well be so. The Christ will inaugurate the new world religion, but this will only take place when the transformation of humanity is complete. The process, I would say, is already beginning. The fact that groups throughout the world now are holding the full-moon meditations for instance, is part of the preparation for this new world religion.

The destruction of part of the American mainland, and, not all, but part of the European mainland and other parts of the

200

world—that they will go down and Atlantis come up—is scheduled, but it is scheduled to take place in about 800 to 900 years from now.

How do you know that?

Well, I have been informed. Everything I say tonight I put forward simply for your consideration; I am not being dogmatic about it. But it is so far ahead I am not worried. Shall I say this, I am sure enough of my information, without being dogmatic, not to be worried about the rise of Atlantis and the breakup of the American continent. By the time this takes place the transformation of humanity, mentally speaking, will be so tremendous that mankind will be prepared for this event—the destruction of the form aspect of humanity will be as nothing, and, in any case, limited in extent.

Mankind will no longer, even in the next 100 years, have fear of death. The realisation that the body is simply a vehicle that lasts for a certain time and is replaced by another one will become so everyday to mankind that this fear of death and of destruction of the physical body and of the body of the planet will disappear. They will take a conscious part in manipulating the energy which controls this. This is taking place *now* in a controlled fashion. There is, above Atlantis, or that part which went under, a great etheric centre which holds all in balance, and as that centre is weakened, energetically speaking, in relation to the floor of the ocean, the floor is allowed to rise just so much, and so fast, and no faster. It is not permitted to come up, zoom, like that. It is a slow, three to four inches a year process. It is done under law, under control.

As to the line-up of planets in 1982, astronomers seem to differ about whether such a line-up exists. In any case, I know of no negative reactions which might result if it does.

FINDHORN

22/3/77

Can you say something about the importance of Findhorn?

Findhorn is a Light Centre, of which there are several on the planet. It has an energetic function: it is energetically linked to other centres, some ancient and some new. It is a centre where those who are ready can find—in the kind of living which they and other centres are discovering, or rather, are exploring—the kind of experience which will allow them to manifest the love principle and develop group consciousness. That is the fundamental function of the light centres. In those centres, people are exploring techniques, relationships, for manifesting love and a gradual awareness of group identity and consciousness.

In this coming age the love of God will become manifest in humanity. The innate brotherhood of men as souls will become a fact on the outer plane, for the first time. This is the Plan for the new age. It will be the age of love and brotherhood. These are the conditioning factors behind a place like Findhorn. There are other factors. But these are the major ones; to allow the people in it to gain experience of group living, because it is through group experience that the Aquarian dispensation will be lived. It is only in group formation that the Aquarian ideas can be sensed, apprehended and worked out. It will be the Age of Synthesis, which is the Age of the Group. Fundamentally, there is only a group in the world—on the soul plane man is One. The Hierarchy is a group. They have no personal, separate consciousness. They only know group consciousness. That kind of quality is being experimented with and given an opportunity for expression in a place like Findhorn. It is also meant to be an example of how a community based on sharing and love illuminates its surroundings and acts like a beacon for others. It has a further, more esoteric role in the future, about which I may not speak.

A very interesting happening on an energetic level is taking place there. A few miles from the community is a very ancient etheric centre on the involutionary arc. Through the help of, and association with, man (the people at Findhorn) the building devas on the evolutionary arc are converting this ancient source of negative (evil because involutionary) energy into positive force. This takes place through the cultivation of the gardens which are such a feature of Findhorn. As trees are planted and agricultural work undertaken in the future, this aspect of the work at Findhorn will expand until the evil energy is transmuted.

Krishnamurti

10/5/77

Early in the century it was officially announced by the Theosophical Society that Krishnamurti was going to be the agent of the Lord Maitreya. Can you comment on this?

He was thought by certain members, Leadbeater and Annie Besant, in particular, to be the coming Christ, the World Teacher. He had certain inner experiences and rejected this, dissolved the Order of the Star, etc. He was in fact being prepared—he was one of a small group being so prepared—as a possible vehicle for Maitreya to manifest through. The plan was changed and he was no longer needed in that way. Maitreya decided that He, Himself, would come. Krishnamurti has now become a great teacher, as you know, with a tremendous following throughout the world.

He might well deny this—it would be in line with his type of thought to deny it—but nevertheless, I would say that Krishnamurti is preparing the way for the Christ's work. He is only one, one of many, who are preparing humanity, but he in his particular manner, is preparing people psychologically, I would say, for the first and second Initiations.

Sai Baba

10/1/78

There is one in India at the moment, Sai Baba. Could He be the Christ?

Sai Baba. Fantastic man. He is a wonderful man, what is called a Spiritual Regent. If I am correct the Christ came into the modern world on July 19th 1977, and Sai Baba has been in the world for quite a number of years now, so He is not the Christ; but he too, in his marvellous way, is preparing mankind for the Christ's work, releasing the principle of Love in the world.

U.F.O.'s

I have heard it said that the Christ will come in a U.F.O.

I, too, have heard it said with great seriousness that the Christ will come in a flying saucer—a U.F.O. I personally do not believe this to be the case. I have said tonight, I always do, that the Christ is Head of *this* planetary Hierarchy. He is in a physical body now in the Himalayas—in a great centre of energy—and so He has no need to come in a flying saucer.

He will come in an aeroplane and the prophecy, that He will come in the clouds, will be fulfilled in this way. He will come in a body of manifestation which is being specially prepared by Him—which He has been preparing for several years—and which is now nearing completion.

Is there any relationship between the Unidentified Flying Objects and the Masters?

All the Hierarchies, of all planets, are in communication. The Hierarchy of this planet is in constant communication, telepathically, with the Hierarchies of other planets. It is an occult fact that all the planets are inhabited. They are not necessarily inhabited by people we would recognise in a physical body; for instance, on Mars or Venus they are in etheric matter and the U.F.O.'s are in fact of etheric substance. When we see them, or when they land, they bring down the vibrational rate of that etheric matter to a lower rate, temporarily, so that we can see them as being solid physical. If you met a Martian or a Venusian—and there could be one in this room now—they would seem just like any of us. That would be a temporary manifestation on the physical plane.

205

There is a definite relationship, in the sense that all the Hierarchies in this solar system work together, and what we call the U.F.O.'s (the vehicles of the space people, from the higher planets) have a very definite part to play in the building of a spiritual platform for the World Teacher, preparing humanity for this time. In fact, since the war, they have played a major role in preserving this planet intact. There have been several times since the war when we have been on the point of destroying the planet by initiating a major war which could annihilate mankind and actually destroy the planet itself, as an integral entity. The space people have placed around this planet a great ring of Light, which holds it intact and protects it from an overflow of force from the cosmic astral plane; negative cosmic evil. The Forces of Evil on this planet gain their energy from the cosmic astral plane. We are protected from too great an overflow of this on to the planet. Our Hierarchy, too, plays a major role in this work. They work very closely together.

They work through Law; economically and lawfully. There is no interference in this world by the U.F.O.'s. It is all done according to law, with the strictest control as to energy and energy distribution.

I predict that you will see over the coming months and the next couple of years, a tremendous increase in U.F.O. activity all over the world—it is already beginning to take place—preparatory to the reappearance of the Christ and the externalisation of the Hierarchy, which is going on at the same time. The two are working in very close rapport. The Space People release into our world tremendous cosmic energies which have a great effect in transforming humanity and in sustaining the planet as an integral being. Their work is continuous and endless, and we all owe them a tremendous debt.

That does not mean to say that they are going to land *en masse*. The Space People are so far advanced, scientifically, that we could not use, now, what they have to give us. It will be 75–125 years before we will be anything like ready to use the information on a technical or scientific level. But in this coming time, startirg from now, you will see a complete reorientation in our attitudes towards the Space People.

206

We will recognise where they come from. We will accept the fact that all the planets are inhabited, that all the planets have their Hierarchies and that these Hierarchies are in communication. We will accept the fact that we are brothers and friends, brothers within one integrated system—the Solar System; that we are all at different stages of evolutionary development, some more advanced and some less. Gradually, we shall take our place, a place which we once held, in the cosmic brotherhood.

Consciously, mankind will see itself as part of this interplanetary brotherhood. We shall work together, and when the time is right—when our science, under the stimulation of the Masters of the Hierarchy, has reached the point where we can utilise what the Space People can show us—they will come and live and work with us for longer periods, and release their great, divine science (it is a divine science) into the world.

24/2/77

How can they appear and disappear again the way they do?

An essential fact to bear in mind in relation to U.F.O.s is that they are etheric in nature. They are etheric physical, not dense physical. What we see is the result of their ability to lower the vibrational rate of themselves, or their vehicles, temporarily, to a level where we can see them and know them. The phenomenon of their disappearing is the shift of their vibrational rate up again. This is something which the Masters, too, can do. Those who have control over matter can do this. It is not all that difficult, I believe, when you know how! It is just the knowing how!

17/5/77

The space people are not nature spirits are they?

Not at all.

Will they look after us?

"Look after" is not quite the word, I would say. They protect us within karmic law. They can go so far and no further, of course.

207

But for the work of the Initiates and the disciples in the world, giving them the karmic right to "interfere", they could do little. With the Christ and the Senior members of our Hierarchy working outwardly in the world, however, a much closer and more open liaison with the Space Brothers becomes possible.

24/2/77

Are any of the space people evil?

The planets are of two kinds. Those which are sacred planets, and those which are non-sacred. The earth is not one of the sacred planets. It is only in the middle of its fourth round, fourth incarnation, you might say, and has not yet undergone that great cosmic Initiation which is the correspondence, in cosmic terms, of the Transfiguration Initiation in man. A man is not truly divine until he has taken that third Initiation, which from the Hierarchical point of view, is the first. Likewise, in cosmos, a planet is not sacred until the Logos has taken the higher correspondence of this Initiation. Sacred planets have no evil.

Mars is a planet which has three levels or zones—zones A, B, and C. Zone A is very advanced, has beings who are very advanced indeed. Zone B, has beings who are really quite advanced. Zone C has beings whom you would not want to meet on a dark night! Notwithstanding, the kind of evil there is not of the same kind as we get on this planet, because the planet Mars as a whole is within the mainstream of the Will of God, so to speak. Mars is also in the middle round, its fourth round, is not a sacred planet, and so it has evil. This lower-zone evil can be very effective, very nasty and disruptive, but speaking broadly and generally, the planet Mars, although its effect on Earth can be disruptive, is within the Plan. Mars is consciously on the Path, in a way that we are not. Hierarchy is in touch of course, but humanity as a whole on this planet, has lost contact. We do not even believe that other planets are inhabited, let alone that we have any contact with them. And yet contact is possible, through the medium of mind. Contact is possible throughout cosmos through the common denominator of mind, if the consciousness is high enough. But of course, it is only the very highest Beings Who have this cosmic consciousness. (Telepathy is a fact, an inborn fact in nature, a natural part of man's being.) Evil on other planets exists, but it is contained in a way that evil on this planet is not so easily contained.

They don't feel evil towards us, for instance. . . ?

Well yes, they do their job as best they can, along their line, but we are protected; it is all under law. There was a time when quite dark entities from planets which we might think are very advanced, could come here on their own volition. They did contact quite a lot of people and this went on for some time. This has been stopped. The contacts made on this planet are governed by law, and there is not this individual kind of contact now.

It is hard to explain this, and I am not sure that I understand it fully, but it is an evil that is different in tension and kind. There is cosmic evil of the worst possible kind; it does work and tries to overflow on to higher levels. This has happened on this planet, as elsewhere. But notwithstanding, the bulk of the planetary citizens are in touch with God. They know the way. They have their bad boys, but they have not lost their way as a planet. We have lost our way, we have literally gone back, and we need help. They give help.

4/10/77

How do we affect the other planets?

The reality is that this planet, and humanity on this planet, are part of a Brotherhood which embraces the whole of the solar system, and each is closely inter-related. The energy from this planet streams into every other planet, and the energy from every other planet streams into all planets, including this one. It is a close energetic co-relationship.

We have to realise this, and that our thoughts and actions create an effect on the aura of this planet which in turn affects every other planet in this system. If we are responding in a certain way, so that the light and energy emitted from this planet is at a relatively low vibration, we are holding up the advancement of the solar system as a whole.

What do you think of all this space exploration, of man going to the Moon?

I love space exploration; I think it's a great thing. What space exploration has done for mankind is to begin the process of realisation that we are only one tiny centre in a huge solar system which itself is a tiny centre in a great galaxy, a fantastic Entity, which we call "space". We have made the first step into this realisation by sending our space rockets to the moon and other planets. We are beginning to realise ourselves as part of a family, and the intense interest which has grown in what are generally called "U.F.O.'s" is an aspect of this too.

Mankind is beginning to realise that it is not alone in the universe, not alone in the solar system. The space people are *our brothers*. We are part of a family which embraces the whole of the solar system, not necessarily on the same plane of manifestation as we are. In fact, the matter aspect of the different planets varies. For instance, if you went to Venus you would see nothing. Venus is inhabited, but our highest etheric energy is their lowest. They start where we leave off.

I thought that the American N.A.S.A. and the Russians were creating pollution and upsetting the ecological balance of the world, aren't they?

No. In fact the advance of the space programmes, in both Russia and America, has only been possible by the direct impression of the minds of the scientists by Hierarchy; not only our Hierarchy, but by the Hierarchy of some higher planets as well. So, you see, it is exactly along the line of Hierarchical planning that this takes place.

24/2/77

Are the governments of the world frightened of the fact of the U.F.O.'s and keeping us in the dark about it?

It is interesting that Mr. Carter, in his run-up to the election, promised, as part of the usual election promises, to release the classified information held by the State Department and the Defence Department in America, and we understand that this is now being de-classified and will be released. So this should release an enormous amount of information which undoubtedly exists about the U.F.O. phenomenon in America.

I myself have seen the files of classified information on U.F.O.'s at our own Air Ministry (not their contents!). There is no doubt that they have a great many reports from Air Force Personnel, who, I know, are forbidden to speak about their experiences. The official line is that the U.F.O.'s do not present a threat to the defence of this country and that therefore the government has no reason to be concerned about them. This, of course, is tantamount to admitting: (a) that the U.F.O.'s exist, and (b) that they are friendly. I would not say they were necessarily frightened of the fact of the U.F.O.'s. I think they are really at a loss as to how to handle this phenomenon.

Would you say this is somehow linked with new contact with outer space?

Oh, indeed, very much. The Hierarchies of all the planets work together. They are, if they want to be, in constant telepathic communication. The U.F.O.'s, the vehicles of certain higher planets, are here on what is basically a spiritual mission. Part of that mission is to hold this planet intact until the Forces of Light reach an energetic balance. This has been achieved. There was a period between 1956, roughly, and late 1959, when this world stood at the crossroads. The future of the world was really in the balance, and all efforts by Hierarchy and by the Hierarchy of some of the higher planets, especially Mars and Venus, were used to offset the mounting evil which was, in a sense, exploding on the planet—the last effort of the forces of evil to prevent the inauguration of the spiritual age of Aquarius; to prevent the externalisation of the Hierarchy and the Reappearance of the Christ.

A great amount of other work is done—the neutralising of large amounts of the negative nuclear radiation in our

211

atmosphere, in our rivers, reservoirs and oceans—which otherwise would have poisoned the planet. The planet is to some extent poisoned, but it would be unliveable in now, but for the work of our space brothers.

The Deva (Angel) Evolution

26/9/75

How do the devas affect us? And could you explain the relationship between us and them?

This is very complicated. The evolution known in the East as the Deva evolution is known to us as the angel evolution, and it is parallel to the human. There are many different deva hierarchies and many very different types of devas, both sub-human and super-human. It is an occult fact that all life-streams on this planet are on the way to being human, or are on the way out of being human; have been human or gone beyond human. The human stage is the central stage through which all lower stages go on the way to higher. There is a very close relationship between some aspects of the deva evolution and the human, in the sense that the human evolution is positive and the deva's is negative. At some point in the far, far distant future it is part of the Divine Plan that these two evolutions should come together. We will then have the divine hermaphrodite—the positive male human aspect and the negative female deva aspect will come together in the one body.

Does the sun and the moon have any connection with this?

The moon provides what we call the negative in the sense of the forces of materiality. They are the forces of our lower nature, whereas the sun provides the forces of our higher nature. The tiny individual devas which make up the vehicle of the human soul, the causal body, come from the sun. They are called solar pitris. The lunar pitris make up our lower bodies, so you have a positive and a negative relationship. The deva evolution and the human evolution will come together closer and closer and we

212

shall work very closely together in the coming age. Already, any Initiate of a certain degree works with the deva evolution, and gradually mankind will learn to work with the healing devas, with the violet devas and green devas, who will teach him how to heal etherically. You know that we have a physical body and a counterpart to this physical body which is made up of the etheric matter of the planet. This, our etheric body, is in, and extends beyond, our physical body. When we get ill it is first of all on the etheric level and gradually we get ill as a correspondence of that, on the physical level; and so from the point of view of healing, you work first of all on the etheric level. This is now beginning to happen—the doctors, scientists, and research workers in the world are now beginning to explore very seriously this etheric plane of matter which is now becoming very much of a reality to many people. When we begin to work closely with the deva evolution they will show us how to control our etheric body, how to heal it, how to bring it into a state of equilibrium and keep it there; and a very close, definite rapport will take place between these two evolutions, quite apart from the long distance aim of becoming ONE.

There are groups of Devas with which man has no direct contact, but which play a crucial role in transmitting to us prana from the sun. Without these Devic lives and Humanity itself, this planet would die. Both are clearing houses of energy for the lower kingdoms.

4/4/78

I remember you once saying that if there were no humanity on the earth, there would be no other form of life on the earth. Well how can that be? Surely other forms of life have existed before man existed on the earth?

There was a time when man was on the moon. The "man in the moon" is a reality. In fact, man was on the moon before he was on the earth.

Not in dense physical form?

Not in dense physical form.

Certain high devas too, were on the moon. They act, with man, as the transmitters of energy from the sun to the lower kingdoms—to the animal, vegetable and mineral kingdom—to the physical body of the planet itself. They vitalise, in a way which only these devas and mankind can vitalise—through the transmission of prana—the lower kingdoms. Without man, and without these particular devas, the lower kingdoms would die.

But would the devas die if we were not here?

They would not. Part of the function of these devas is to transmit prana to us. So their function would be disturbed, there would be an energetic over-balance. The prana would be there. They would be there. They would transmit prana—but to what? The animal kingdom? They would kill off all the animal kingdom. Unless we step down the energy through us to them the animal kingdom would die. Tonight we stepped down, from a very high level, the spiritual energy—we act as transformers by transmitting it. It goes into the world at a lower voltage and therefore is more acceptable, more accessible, more usable, by mankind.

If the energy from the sun passed through the high devas but not through humanity, there would be a stage where it was not transformed. The bodies of the animal kingdom are not refined enough to accept the prana at the level which it would receive from the devas and they would gradually die out.

But what about before man was on the earth in a physical body?

He was in etheric matter. Before mankind was physical, there were two races of etheric man, who performed the same function. They weren't true men but they performed the same function for the lower kingdoms.

When man came into incarnation in Lemurian times, on the physical plane, through the heightening of the vibration of his physical body which this entailed, gradually more and more of the higher fires—because this is what it is—from the sun were able to be transmitted. And so the evolutionary process could take place. Man is no longer on the moon so the moon is a dead carcass—a decaying carcass in the heavens. This is why it is malefic to men.

The comet Kahoutek

5/3/76

Do you feel that the comet Kahoutek was bringing in disintegrating energies, to accelerate the disintegration of all our established institutions, or that it was, say, a manifestation of the Hierarchy, sending in energies . . .?

Not disintegrating energies, but on the contrary, great synthesising forces were released by this comet as it passed through our Solar System; synthesising forces which will have a tremendous effect on this planet, as on all the other planets. This Solar System will progress enormously as a result of the inflow of this comet with its synthesising energies. This is part of the Initiatory process which is taking place.

27/1/76

If you leave the planet, where might you go? Does organic life exist on the different levels in the Hierarchy?

All the planets are inhabited. If a Master leaves this planet, He might go to a higher planet. Or as many of Them do, to Sirius, which is the real source of our planetary Hierarchy; our Hierarchy is a branch of the Great White Brotherhood on Sirius. In fact the relationship between this solar system and Sirius is the same kind of relationship, on a cosmic level, as your personality has to its soul. So you can understand what that relationship is.

There are seven different ways the Masters can take after They have taken the fifth initiation. This is called the Way of the Higher Evolution. There is the Way to become a Heavenly Man—a Logos. You train to become a Logos. Perhaps you, one day, will become a Logos. You can ensoul a planet. Or you might become an expression of the Son aspect of God, the

215

Cosmic Christ. The Cosmic Christ is an Identity, an Individuality, Who has been man at one time. Just as the planetary Christ is a man, a divine man because He has manifested this very divinity we are talking about, which is potential within every one of us—from the lowest savage up to the Christ Himself. Everyone is divine. We all stem from the same divine source—but are all at different stages in that journey back. The Masters and the Initiates are away ahead of us. They are coming now to help us so that humanity can take this tremendous step forward into the beginning of Initiate consciousness.

ANCIENT CIVILISATIONS

27/1/76

What signs do you see of evolution over the past, say, few thousand years—in man's evolution as a whole?

Oh, Leonardo da Vinci, Schweitzer, Beethoven, Plato, Shakespeare, Galileo, Abraham Lincoln, one could go on and on. The emergence of these Initiates, for that is what they are, is a sign of man's evolution, as are all the arts, all the great scientific revelations. The exploration of the atom; the discovery that matter is energy; that you can release energy from the building blocks of nature itself, this is incredible—this is the great science. And when we learn to handle it safely, and for the good of all, instead of for negative purposes, this energy will give us a base on which to build a civilisation beyond our imagination.

The spread of knowledge—an almost universal educational programme—and world-wide communications, with the sense of Oneness which this engenders, has brought humanity today to the point of readiness for the new Revelation which the Christ brings.

A Golden Age—Atlantis

1/2/77

Is there another Golden Age coming?

Indeed, yes. A golden age. A diamond age. An age of the manifestation of divine qualities in Man which have never manifested before. The golden age in mankind's communal psyche was the age of the Atlantean civilisation. Atlantis had a science more advanced than we have today; a science of building which we cannot rival; a spiritual science which we have not even begun to manifest. But in this coming age we will not only rival but surpass that civilisation's science which was given as a gift to mankind by Hierarchy. Humanity did not make it. They did not have the mental development to make it. The Fourth Race, the Atlantean, had as a goal, the perfecting of the astral or emotional body—bringing that to a state of sensitivity and responsiveness which we take as normal. In fact it is so developed that we have the greatest difficulty in mastering it now. Most of humanity are still Atlantean in the sense that the masses of mankind are astrally polarised. The focus of their attention is the emotional body; the energy from the astral plane is that which most potently works through them and they live from the solar plexus.

Through the evolutionary process, and through meditation and service, the more advanced units of the race are beginning to be or are already mentally polarised, or focused. Today, large sections of mankind, for the first time in history, are beginning to think, truly to think for themselves; to actually use the energy of mind and make conscious choices and decisions. Up to now, mankind as a whole simply reacted. Thinking is something, as we know, which is entirely different.

The masses of mankind are beginning to think—politically, economically—they are beginning to take decisions along these lines, and no longer simply respond emotionally to some teacher or some leader. This is new.

In Atlantean days mankind did not think at all. Only the most advanced Atlantean man, the disciple or Initiate, thought. In mid-Atlantean times, the highest Initiation that could be taken was what is now the Third Initiation. (St. Paul was a third degree Initiate so we have some idea what a third degree Initiate of His time might be like.) Third degree Initiates today, of course, are much more mentally developed than in St. Paul's time. It is harder to become a third degree Initiate now, a much tougher assignment, because mankind has developed so much mentally. A higher quality of Initiate is being created all the time: the Masters of today would have been tremendous Adepts in Atlantean times. The Christ and the Buddha were among the very earliest of our earth humanity to take the third Initiation in mid-Atlantean times, and have been at the forefront of our evolution ever since. They are great Planetary Lives, unbelievably advanced as far as we are concerned.

In Atlantean times the Hierarchy were from other planets, not from our own earth humanity—or were just beginning to be. The most advanced humans were just beginning to become Initiate.

The Atlantean civilisation covered an enormous span of time, of course, and for long was uncorrupted, at a high spiritual peak. It was a Golden Age.

Then the Lords of the Dark Face and the Lords of the Light, the Hierarchy of Light, came into direct opposition, as the forces of evil ceased to restrict their activity to the realm where it is right, which is on the plane of matter. The work of the forces of evil, which are really the forces of involution on the planet, is to uphold the matter aspect. They are on the involutionary arc, while we are on the evolutionary arc; we are moving out of matter. Their activity is inimical to us, but it has its part to play in the involutionary development of the planet. Where their activity overflows on to the evolutionary arc and affects mankind, it is evil—the dominance of the minds and hearts and activity of mankind, which is what they seek to achieve. They have their adepts who are very advanced—as advanced along their line as the Masters are along Theirs. Only, they have not the energy of love; the love nature is missing from their make-up. Eventually, in the course of time—hundreds of thousands of years from now—they will go through the cycles, manifest the energy of love, and come into the unfoldment of the Christ Consciousness.

It is their activity on the physical and astral realms which holds mankind back. Also, the fact that this planet is not a perfect Being. It is a very imperfect planet. From the cosmic point of view this planet is only at the stage of a second degree Initiate—not yet fully divine. You become truly divine only when you take the third Initiation, the first true soul Initiation. Up till then, there is simply a personality integration. It is more than that—but to oversimplify—it is a personality integration which takes place; from the Hierarchical point

219

of view, the third Initiation is the true first Initiation.

This planet is not what is called a sacred planet. In Theosophical terminology, there are seven rounds through which each planet has to go; seven incarnations—our planet is in the middle of the fourth. We have a long way to go. But in the middle of the fourth all the new, great spiritual possibilities arise.

Yes, under the inspiration of the Christ and the Masters we shall create a golden age—and by our own hands this time.

4/10/76

But have these other civilisations not had the same help from Hierarchy that we have now?

Yes. The Atlantean civilisation was given to man by the Hierarchy. Atlantean man did not build that brilliant civilisation, which in many ways was far more advanced than our own, scientifically. They had electro-magnetic weapons which destroyed the civilisation. They had a most advanced science, a wonderful civilisation, but it was given as a gift by the Hierarchy of the time, the Masters and Initiates of the time. Atlantean man was much less evolved than we are, in many ways.

Can we say that this gift destroyed Atlantean man?

This gift did not destroy them. They misused it, through their free-will. Man is given free-will. From that point on the Hierarchy became occult, esoteric, retreated into the desert and mountain areas of the world, where Their successors, the Masters of today, still live. Some are the same Beings—you wouldn't believe it possible. The Manu of the Fifth Root race has been the Manu for nearly 100,000 years. And the Manu, the second of two, for the Fourth Root race, the Atlantean, is still in the world, in China. How old He would be I just couldn't imagine—hundreds of thousands of years.

We are perfecting the mental vehicle, whereas Atlantean man was perfecting the astral vehicle, which is now perfected.

Humanity is, today, totally different from even 2,000 years ago. Then, the Christ, manifesting through the Disciple Jesus, spoke to uneducated, superstitious peasants, shepherds and fishermen, who were dominated by the priests, whose one concern was to keep their hold over the minds of the people. Today, as the result of the Piscean experience, of world-wide education, of the tremendous speed-up and dissemination of the means of communication—press, radio, television, books, trains, air transport, and so on—mankind is increasingly independent. The Christ is coming into an entirely different kind of world. Mankind is now adult. Humanity, the world disciple, has grown up.

Large sections of humanity are now standing on the very threshold of the First Initiation—into the kind of consciousness which the Initiates and the Masters know; the first step. In this coming fifty years even, hundreds of thousands of people will take this first Initiation—and that is something extraordinary. Mankind has made an enormous advance. The Hierarchy will be back in the world. The Christ will be in the world. Mankind has the possibility now of entering an entirely new spiritual age and of building a civilisation greater than any known before—greater than the Atlantean or any subsequent civilisation. We have the chance. Inevitably, *we* have to do it. But we are ready to do it. We have the capacity to do it. Under the guidance of the Masters, we shall build a civilisation based on brotherhood, love, right sharing, right relationship to each other and to God. This is the right basis. This is where the Atlantean civilisation fell apart.

There grew up those who were not content with the Will of God, and asserted their own separated will. The result was disaster. This time the forces of darkness will not succeed in bringing humanity to such straits. They are already defeated.

Egypt and Atlantis

28/2/77

You mentioned Atlantis in your talk. Is there any connection between Egypt and Atlantis, say perhaps through reincarnation or other historical means?

Yes. Egypt was a late colony of the Atlantean civilisation which covered a large part of the world. The Great Pyramid of Cheops in Egypt is far older than we imagine—the civilisation of Egypt is far older—in fact, below the area around the Great Pyramid and the Sphinx is a city, a colonial Atlantean city, which one day will be excavated and revealed.

The Sphinx, and of course, the Pyramid, were connected with the Ancient Mysteries, the Mysteries of Initiation, for Initiation and the Mystery Schools go back to Atlantean times. The process of Initiation was instituted in mid-Atlantean times, and the remains in Egypt, South America—Mexico and Peru—and also in Chaldea and Babylon, relate to these ancient civilisations. They are degenerated forms of it, for the Atlantean civilisation was a tremendous, scientific civilisation, such as the world has not seen since.

In Egypt, the requirements of Initiation were known, but occultly; there was no outer teaching as there is today. The ancient religion of Atlantis was what today we call spiritualism. It was the recognition and the worship of the fact—worship is not quite the right word—the recognition of the *sacredness* of the fact of everlasting life. So that when someone died, the afterlife was for the Atlantean as important and was prepared for; burial had a very specific ritual. You find this wherever the Atlantean civilisation colonised itself and remained for some time, as it did in Egypt.

The religion of ancient Egypt is, fundamentally, Spiritualism; the religion of China, for the last 4,000 years, is a kind of Spiritualism. We call it Ancestor Worship, but of course it has nothing to do with ancestor *worship*. It is the worship of the fact of the sacredness of life continuing after death—that continuity of life—so that the ancestors co-exist with the men and women of today; the recognition and acceptance of that fact.

This is the core of the ancient Atlantean and Egyptian religions; hence the apparent over-emphasis on death, the almost morbid interest, even today, in South America, in the trappings of death. (But the South American peasants see a lot of death. They are very familiar with it. They are poor. Most of the coffins are very small—for children, who die in large numbers. These people live closely with death through no fault of their own. It is largely because of non-distribution of the food and modern medical knowledge that their children die.)

Egypt was the home of magic—Atlantean magic. The burials in the tombs, and later in the Pyramids, were magically performed. They were closed, sealed, magically; and, in fact, there are tombs today in Egypt which have been unopened, and cannot be opened, until the magical "seal" is removed. They have been set in place by words of power and certain rituals which will not allow their disturbance without the "codeword" to release the power of the mantram.

This was also the magic of Atlantis, black and white. Black magic was tremendously rampant in Atlantean times, and of course you know that there was a great war, between the forces of Light and Darkness, which brought that civilisation to an end. As a result of that war the Hierarchy of Light became occult. They removed Themselves from the everyday world to Their mountain and desert retreats, leaving mankind to fend for itself, and to learn through trial and error. They return now among us, one by one.

4/10/76

Is this energy really going to make an enormous step forward this time, because there have been civilisations before ours far more advanced than we are now, and they have fallen, and one doesn't understand why, if all this is a plan for earth, why have these better civilisations that we have now, collapsed?

Because of man's free-will. Man is divine. He is also human and he has free-will. And he is given the chance to exert that free-will. Humanity must evolve out of its sense of what is right for it; has to bring its will into line with the divine will, which issues from Shamballa, where the Will of God is known. When the will of man and the Will of God coincide, you have right living—the Plan goes forward. There are no downfalls. When you have a divergence of man's will from God's Will for long enough, disaster comes. In the better civilisations you are

223

thinking of, the Atlantean, men grew selfish, exerted their little self-will, and the eventual result was disaster.

This time, man is far more evolved, is much more an adult, mental unit, and can make decisions as to his future in the light of the evidence which will be highlighted for him by the Christ. He will see that there is no alternative today to sharing and co-operation, and on that basis will go into the future.

SELECTED MESSAGES FROM MAITREYA, THE CHRIST

Message No. 2

September 15th 1977

Good evening, My dear friends.

I have taken, again, this opportunity to speak to you, and to establish firmly in your minds the reasons for My return.

There are many reasons why I should descend and appear once more among you.
Chiefly they are as follows:

My Brothers, the Masters of Wisdom, are scheduled to make Their group return to the everyday world.
As Their Leader, I, as one of Them, do likewise.

Many there are throughout the world who call Me, beg for My return.
I answer their pleas.

Many more are hungry and perish needlessly, for want of the food which lies rotting in the storehouses of the world.

Many need My help in other ways: as Teacher, Protector; as Friend and Guide.

It is as all of these I come.

To lead men, if they will accept Me, into the New Time, the New Country, the glorious future which awaits humanity in this coming Age;

For all of this I come.

I come too, to show you the Way to God, back to your Source; to show you that the Way to God is a simple path which all men can tread;

To lead you upwards, into the Light of that new TRUTH which is the REVELATION that I bring.

For all of this I come.

Let me take you by the hand and lead you into that beckoning Country, to show you the marvels, the glories of God, which are yours to behold.

The vanguard of My Masters of Wisdom are now among you.
Soon you will know Them.
Help Them in Their work.
Know too, that They are building the New Age, through you.
Let Them lead and guide, show you the way; and in doing this you will have served your brothers and sisters well.

Take heart, My friends.
All will be well.
All manner of things will be well.

Good night, My dear friends.

May the Divine Light and Love and Power of the One God be now manifest within your hearts and minds.
May this manifestation lead you to seek That which dwells ever within you.
Find That, and know God.

Message No. 10

November 8th 1977

I am among you once more, My dear friends.

I come to tell you that you will see Me very soon, each in his own way.
Those who look for Me in terms of My beloved Disciple, the Master Jesus, will find His qualities in Me.
Those who look for Me as a Teacher are nearer the mark, for that is what I am.
Those who search for signs will find them, but My method of manifestation is more simple.

Nothing separates you from Me, and soon many will realise this.
I am with you and in you.
I seek to express that which I am through you;
for this I come.

Many will follow Me and see Me as their Guide.
Many will know Me not.
My aim is to enter into the life of all men and through them change that life.
Be ready to see Me soon;
be ready to hear My words,
to follow My thoughts, .
to heed My plea.

I am the Stranger at the Gate.
I am the One Who knocks.
I am the One Who will not go away.

I am your Friend.
I am your Hope.
I am your Shield.
I am your Love.
I am All in All.

Take Me into yourselves, and let Me work through you.
Make Me part of yourselves, and show Me to the world.
Allow Me to manifest through you, and know God.

May the Divine Light and Love and Power of the One and Holy God be now manifest within your hearts and minds.
May this manifestation lead you to know that God dwells silently, now and forever, within you all.

Message No. 17

February 14th 1978

Good evening, My dear friends, I am happy to be with you once more, in this way.

Soon My Appearance will be known to many and My Teaching will have begun.
Mankind will be faced by Me with two lines of action: on their decision rests the future of this world.
I will show them that the only possible choice is through sharing and mutual interdependence. By this means, Man will come into that state of awareness of himself and his purpose which will lead him to the feet of God.
The other way is too terrible to contemplate, for it would mean the annihilation of all life-streams on this Earth.

Man has the future in his hands.
Weigh well, oh Men, and if you choose as True Men would, I may lead you into the Light of your Divine inheritance.
Make your choice well and let Me lead.
Make your choice well and be assured of my continuing succour.
Make your choice well, My brothers, and be delivered of all that holds you in limitation.

My Army is on the move, is marching bravely into the future.
Join those who already fight on the side of Light, on the side of Truth, of Freedom and Justice.
Join My Vanguard and show the way for your brothers.

Many there are who sense that I am here, yet speak not. Why hold this knowledge to yourselves when your brothers cry for light, for wisdom, and help?
Allow them, too, to share in the joy of the Promise which I bring.
Tell them, My friends, that you believe that Maitreya has come;

231

that the Lord of Love is here;
that the Son of Man walks again among His brothers.
Tell them that soon My Face will be seen, My Words will be heard;
and in the seeing and the hearing they are tested and known.

May the Divine Light and Love and Power of the One Most Holy God be now manifest within your hearts and minds.
May this manifestation lead you to seek and to find that Divine Source from which you came.

Message No. 19

February 28th 1978

Good evening, My dear friends, I am happy indeed to be with you once more and to tell you that I emerge forthwith.

The time of My Coming is over.
The time of My emergence has arrived and soon, now, in full vision and fact, My Face and Words will become known.
May you quickly recognise Me, My dear friends, My dear ones, and help your brothers to do likewise.

I am your Friend and Brother, not a God.
It is true My Father has, once again, sent Me to you, but I come to you who are My Brethren, to guide you and lead you, if you will, into a blessed future.
My task will be to show that for mankind the Ways part.
The Signposts are set and on your decision rests the future of this Earth.
We are here together, you and I, to ensure that Man chooses the correct path, the only Way which can lead him to God.

You are here because in your heart you are responding to My Call, to the fact of My Presence, knowingly or not.
Make it then your task to tell the others, to point to the simple way of Truth which beckons mankind.
Teach men that to share is divine;
to love is God's nature;
to work together is Man's destiny.
Take your stand on the only platform from which the Light of the future may be seen.
Take your stand My friends, together, and show the Way.

Many of you will see Me soon.
Share with your brothers this joyous expectation and tell them that Maitreya, their Friend, their Brother, their Teacher of old, has come.

233

Do this now and restore to men the hope which they have lost.
Do this now and work for Me.
Work in service to the world and stand in the Blessing of My Love.

May the Divine Light and Love and Power of the One most Holy God be now manifest within your hearts and minds.
May this manifestation reveal to you that you are, now and forever, sons of the only living God.

Message No. 26

April 18th 1978

My dear friends, I am happy to be with you once more.

I am indeed among you, in a new way: your brothers and sisters know Me, have seen Me and call Me friend and brother.

My Plan is to reveal Myself stage by stage, and to draw together around Me those enlightened souls through whom I may work. This process has begun, and soon, in My Centre, My Presence will become known.

My body of workers will show the world that the problems of Mankind can be solved: through the process of sharing and just redistribution the needs of all can be met.
This growing group will show men that there is but little need for the suffering of so many: for the hunger, disease and anguish which beset mankind.

My Plan is to take you on a journey into a New Country, a new approach to living in which all men can share.
Let Me lead you, let Me show you the way, let Me lift you upwards into the Light of a new Truth;
let Me show you, My friends, the Way to God, for only through the manifestation of God's Will can God be known.
I am here to administer that Will.

Take this opportunity to serve and grow in service, My friends, for none greater has been offered to any man.
Take this opportunity to serve, and see the Face of Him we call God.

My arms are held towards you, My friends, asking for your trust, appealing for your help in remaking your world.
Many are the tasks which lie ahead, many are the blows which must be struck for Freedom and Truth.

I need all those in whom that Truth shines to follow Me and help Me in My work.

May you be ready when you hear My Call. That Call will resound in the ears of men everywhere, throughout the world. It is a Call to God.

May the Divine Light and Love and Power of the One Most Holy God be now manifest within your hearts and minds.

May this manifestation lead you to seek and to know that Essence of God which in Truth you are.

Message No. 35

July 6th 1978

My dear friends, I am happy to be with you once more.

My Plans work out. My Emergence takes a little time but proceeds well. Soon, among your brothers, My Teaching will begin and, resounding through the world, will usher in a New Age.

My Promise holds: I shall take before the throne of God all who can follow Me into the Higher Light which I bring. May you be among those who shall know this joy.
Take your place by My side and together shall we make all things new.
Take My hand, My friends, and let Me guide you through My Garden.
Let Me show you My Flowers.
Let Me teach you My Law.

My Heart enfolds you as always and on each step of the upward path My Hand steadies and guides.
I am your Master, Brother and Friend. Know Me then in this way.
Let Me show you the simple Path to God.
Let Me show you the Greater Light Divine.
Let us travel together this Path and know
the Secrets of Old,
know the Wonders of God,
know the Blessing of Love.

The cry for Justice from men has reached My ears and to that cry I hearken.
The call for succour has risen to Me and I hasten to give.
The pain of the world sits heavily on My heart and this gladly would I lighten.
My Pain can be yours; My Burden can be shared. I offer you both.

Take My Pain, My brothers, and turn it into Joy.
Ease My Burden, My friends, and know Bliss.

May the Divine Light and Love and Power of the One Most
Holy God be now manifest within your hearts and minds.
May this manifestation lead you to see that you are always and
ever Centres in the Being of God.

Message No. 42

My dear friends, I am happy to be with you once more.

Many times have you heard Me say that My Coming means change.
Specifically, the greatest change will be in the hearts and minds of men, for My Return among you is a sign that men are ready to receive new life.
That New Life for men do I bring in abundance.
On all the planes this life will flow, reaching the hearts and souls and bodies of men, bringing them nearer to the Source of Life Itself.
My task will be to channel those Waters of Life through you.

I am the Water Carrier.
I am the Vessel of Truth.
That Truth shall I reveal to you and lift you into your true nature.

I am the River.
Through Me flows the new stream of God-given Life, and this shall I bestow on you.
Thus shall we together walk through My Garden, smell the perfume of My Flowers, and know the joy of closeness to God.

My friends, these things are not dreams.
All of this will be yours.
My Mission will vouchsafe this to you.

May the Divine Light and Love and Power of the One Most Holy God be now manifest within your hearts and minds.
May this manifestation take you into the Lap of the Everlasting God.

Message No. 53

December 7th 1978

My dear friends, I am happy to be with you once more.

My methods meet with success. My agents work correctly and well, and all proceeds to plan.
My Plan is to remain in My Centre until My Declaration is made.
Then My Progression round the countries of the world will begin, and all men shall see My Face.
When I place Myself before you I shall ask for your allegiance, for your help in service to your brothers.
I know already those on whom I may count.

My task will be to take you on a journey into Truth, into the Blessed Country of Love, and there to show you to yourselves as God.
My Master   likewise, will take you by the hand and lead you to His Divine Feet.

Let us together show the world:
that the need for war is past;
that the instinct of man is to live and to love;
that hatred is begotten of separation;
that the Law of God lives in man and is fundamental to his nature.
All of this shall I show you. Work with Me and prove this to be true.

I am the Conveyor of God's Love.
I am the Administrator of God's Will.
The Light of God dwells in Me and that Light do I turn on you.
Grow therein, My friends, and shine with the Glory of God.

My Plan is to reveal Myself in such a way that few, indeed, will know not who I am.

240

Therefore, watch for My Presence.
Seek out My Face and Words and hearken quickly to them.

My Blessing goes with you all.

May the Divine Light and Love and Power of the One Most
Holy God be now manifest within your hearts and minds.
May this manifestation lead you to be ever mindful of your
likeness to God.

Message No. 61

February 14th 1979

My dear friends, I am happy indeed to be among you once more in this way, and to release to you something of My Plans.

Within the group wherein I dwell are those who know Me for what I am, but it is My intention to withhold for a certain time My true status.
This will enable you to see Me as one of yourselves, a man among men.
Nothing which I do will seem extraordinary.
Nothing which I say will be bizarre or strange.
Simple indeed will be My approach. On this fact you may count.

As a brother among brothers I shall speak for you all, voice aloud your aspirations and hopes;
make known the desire of all men for a world at peace;
for a just and noble readiness to share;
for the creation of a society based on freedom and love.
By My enunciation of these principles will you know and discover Me.

My intention is to reveal Myself soon and by the shortest route.
All else failing, I shall emerge into a world ready but unprepared; a world which knows not yet that I am among you.
But far better would it be for Me to come before you as the Expected One, the One sent by God to lead you into your future glory.
Many know this, but many more by far are ignorant of the true happenings of the time.

I do solemnly appeal to you, therefore, My dear friends, to make known the fact of My Presence among you and pave smooth My Way.

242

My burdens are heavy indeed.
These burdens may be lightened by your work.
I trust you to act and follow.
Together we shall complete the Plan.

My Blessings go with you all.

May the Divine Light and Love and Power of the One Most
Holy God be now manifest within your hearts and minds.
May this manifestation lead you to be ever mindful of your true
purpose as servants of the Plan.

Message No. 70

May 17th 1979

Good evening, My dear friends. Once again I am happy to be among you in this way.

My Plan proceeds carefully and well.
Your brothers grow in number around Me and to them do I give My Blessing and Teaching.
Likewise, in due course, shall I bestow on you these gifts.

My aim is to spread abroad My net to the widest horizon, to draw to Me all those in whom My Light shines, that through them I may work.
This cast can include you, My friends, for I need all who share with Me the desire to serve the world.
Take upon yourselves the task of succour and share My burden.
Share with Me, My friends, in a great work—nothing less than the transformation of this world.

My means, as you know, are simple.
I need no other tools than the heart's love of man.
This, My friends, bestowed on you by That from which you come, will bring men to the Source of Love Itself.
Make it manifest My brothers, and join Our ranks.

I am the Custodian of the Plan of God.
I am the New Direction.
I am the Way for all men.
I hold the Secrets of Old.
I bestow Bliss.
I create the desire for Truth.
I make all men One.
I come to realise My Truth through men.
I am the Saviour of Old.
I am the Teacher of the New.
I am the Guide for the Future Time.

I am the Law Embodied.
I am Truth Itself.
I am your Friend and Brother.
I am your Self.

Take within you That which I am and make That manifest in the world.

Take within you That which I bestow and create the City of Light.

Manifest around you That which I pronounce and become as Gods.

May the Divine Light and Love and Power of the One Most Holy God be now manifest within your hearts and minds. May this manifestation lead you to be encircled by the Aura of God.

Message No. 81

My dear friends, I am happy indeed to be with you once more, and to magnetise your aspiration in this way.

My Coming evokes in man a desire for change, a desire for betterment, however expressed.
My energies engender in man divine discontent.
All that is useless in our structures must go.
There are many such which are unworthy of man today.

Man is an emerging God and thus requires the formation of modes of living which will allow this God to flourish.
How can you be content with the modes within which you now live: when millions starve and die in squalor; when the rich parade their wealth before the poor; when each man is his neighbour's enemy; when no man trusts his brother?
For how long must you live thus, My friends?
For how long can you support this degradation?

My Plan and My duty is to reveal to you a new way, a way forward which will permit the divine in man to shine forth.
Thus do I speak gravely, My friends and brothers. Hearken well to My words.
Man must change or die; there is no other course.
When you see this you will gladly take up My Cause, and show that for man exists a future bathed in Light.

My teaching is simple:
Justice, Sharing and Love are Divine Aspects.
To manifest his divinity man must embrace these three.

May the Divine Light and Love and Power of the One Most Holy God be now manifest within your hearts and minds.
May this manifestation bring you to the realisation of your part in the Great Plan.

Message No. 82

September 18th 1979

My dear friends, I am happy indeed to be among you once more in this fashion, and to set before you some guidelines for the future.

My Task will be to show you how to live together peacefully as brothers.
This is simpler than you imagine, My friends, for it requires only the acceptance of Sharing.
Sharing, indeed, is divine.
It underlies all progress for man.
By its means, My brothers and sisters, you can come into correct relationship with God; and this My friends, underlies your lives.
When you share, you recognise God in your brother.
This is a Truth, simple, but until now difficult for man to grasp.
The time has come to evidence this Truth.

By My Presence the Law of Sharing will become manifest.
By My Presence man will grow to God.
By the Presence of Myself and My Brothers, the New Country of Love shall be known.
Take, My friends, this simple Law to your hearts.
Manifest Love through Sharing, and change the world.
Create around you the atmosphere of Peace and Joy, and with Me make all things new.

My Coming portends change.
Likewise, grief at the loss of the old structures.
But, My friends, the old bottles must be broken—the new wine deserves better.

My friends, My brothers, I am near you now.
I see above and around you your aspiration for Love and Joy.

247

I know this to be widespread in mankind; this makes possible
My return.

Let Me unveil for you your divine inheritance.
Let Me show you the wonders of God which yet await you.
Allow Me to take you simply by the hand and lead you to the
Forest of Love,
the Glade of Peace,
the River of Truth.

Take My hand, My friends, and know this to be yours, now.

May the Divine Light and Love and Power of the One Most
Holy God be now manifest within your hearts and minds.
May this manifestation lead you in trust to the Country I call
Love.

HOW THE PLAN IS WORKING OUT

Now that the Day of Declaration is rapidly approaching, it might be worthwhile to take a closer look at the radical changes which our world is undergoing.

The Hierarchy is planning that Maitreya will be a national figure, in the country where He now resides, within half a year, subsequently to become internationally known within one further year at the latest. The Day of Declaration, therefore, will be about 18 months from now, May 1982.

His presence in our midst since July 1977, must therefore have brought about exceptional changes. It is submitted that these consequences are visible to anyone who examines world events with an open mind.

If what has been said in reply to the many questions posed in previous years is true, there should be signs of an increased interest in the problem of world hunger in political circles and in the media; signs of an unexpected relaxation of tension; and of a gradual decline in the frequency of earthquake activity. Even a superficial study of the international news bears this out.

At the end of 1976 it was predicted (see Political Effects chapter, page 163) that there would be a notable relaxation of tension in Africa and in the Middle East. The closer relations between Egypt and Israel and the completely unexpected easing of the situation in Rhodesia, are the first indications of this.

Further examples are: the International Legal Commission, consultants to the U.N., an organization of some of the most eminent laywers in the world, has named 1979: "a notable year for human rights." The Commission referred to the fact that in Africa three of the most notorious dictators (Amin, Bokassa, Macias) had been overthrown. In Bolivia, Bangla Desh, Ecuador, Ghana, Nigeria and Nicaragua, military regimes were replaced by civil governments.

In several other countries also, among them Indonesia, tens of thousands of political prisoners have been freed.

This information not only confirms that unique events are taking place in the world, but also emphasizes, once again, that changes must occur naturally through the actions of man himself. Maitreya and the Masters can direct spiritual energies to stimulate the development of all manner of plans, but it is up to man to react — and act.

How concrete these reactions already are, can be deduced, amongst other things, from a report of the North-South Commission, of which 18 well known politicians under the chairmanship of the former West German Chancellor Herr Willy Brandt, are a part. Edward Heath, the former Prime Minister of Great Britain, and Olof Palme of Sweden, are members of this Commission.

Maitreya's submission, that the world has only two choices, sharing or total destruction, is dramatically underlined by the Commission. The title of the Brandt report, "A Program for Survival," makes that quite clear. According to the Commission, if we are to avert catastrophe on a global scale, we must radically change our international economic order.

Another report, that of the American Presidential Commission, established recently that 1 out of every 8 people in the world suffers from malnutrition — "seriously enough to shorten the life expectancy, to effect the physical growth, and to blunt the mental capacities." This Commission warned that if measures are not taken very soon, there is likelihood of famine on a world scale within 20 years. Such a famine, says the Commission, would present a much greater problem than the present energy crisis.

A UNICEF report calculated that if every family were to be provided with unpolluted water and adequate sanitary facilities, the results of hunger and malnutrition would be reduced by 80%. That could be realized within ten years at a cost of 9 billion dollars per year. A gigantic sum certainly, but the industrialized nations in only one year spend 100 billion dollars (ten times more) on alcoholic beverages, apart from the 500 billion dollars spent annually on defense.

A brief summary of further facts:

- Sixteen major newspapers together produce a periodic supplement about the new international economic order which is circulated by newspapers in the East and West, the North and the South, under the motto "the world is one."
- The Brazilian archbishop Dom Helder Camera has named hunger as being the underlying cause of every form of violence.
- The Nobel prize winner in Economics, Prof. Dr. J. Tinbergen, has said that the world is in the position of either "surviving together or perishing together."
- More than 1½ million people, mainly in America have, since 1977, joined the Hunger Project whose aim is to impress on everyone that we are all personally responsible for ending world hunger.
- The president of the Council of Ministers of the E.E.C., M. Gaston Thorn, from Luxembourg, has said that his first priority as President of the E.E.C. Commission will be to improve relations with the Third World.
- The head of the Department for Developmental Problems of the World Council of Churches, Dr. Julio de Santa Ana, advocates a very definite stance on the side of the poor: "If the churches still wish to retain any credibility at all in the 1980's, then they must stand unconditionally on the side of the poor and oppressed."
- The Netherlands Prime Minister, Mr. van Agt, appealed to the U.S.A. to take the lead in launching a major international rescue operation to help the starving Third World. He made this appeal in a speech:..."the earth belongs to all men; everyone has the right to the world's resources and the duty to redistribute them internationally."
- In his first speech as president of the Assembly of the U.N. the former German diplomat, Rüdiger von Wechmar, made an urgent appeal to the wealthy western nations to help the developing countries out of their difficulties.
- South Africa has hesitantly, but unmistakably, begun to devote more attention to the rights of her oppressed black population.
- As a result of the fierce criticism levelled at it, the International Monetary Fund has revised its policy in order to more justly represent the interests of the Third World.
- In a very recent report from the American Congress (October 1980), it is stated that there is a very little time left to take measures to avert a global catastrophe due to food shortages. "If we do not act quickly and drastically to change the course of events, it will soon become impossible to prevent destruction on a world scale."

All these statements and developments are signs of a dawning awareness of the position in which our society finds itself; it is indeed a matter of "share or die." In this awareness however, lies the implication that it is still possible to change course. That possibility will become a certainty as soon as man has pledged himself in support of Maitreya.

As foretold in this book (see page 163), there has been a sudden decrease in the frequency and the seriousness of earthquake activity in recent years. In 1976 about 700,000 people perished in earthquakes, mainly in China. In 1977 there were 2,800 victims and 15,915 in 1978. The death toll during the first half of 1979 was 100, according to a report in the Washington Post.

This sudden decrease in earthquake activity, after it had been increasing in intensity and frequency over the last century, can be ascribed to the influence of Maitreya acting as the Agent of Divine Intervention. It is not claimed that there will therefore suddenly be no more earthquakes, the recent disaster in Algeria indicates the contrary. Earthquakes will still occur during the coming years, but to a decreasing extent and with less serious repercussions.

An interesting development in this context occurred in California. Until very recently geological experts all agreed that due to a colossal increase in pressure along the San Andreas fault, the danger of a catastrophe was very great. According to a report in the newspaper, Star News (May 10, 1980), an exploratory team of geologists discovered in December 1979 that something was very wrong: the pressure which was keeping the earth's crust on each side of the fault line together was beginning to force a separation. Geophysicist Barry Raleigh declared that if this continued, it would inevitably, sooner rather than later, result in a major earthquake.

In fact, it was expected that California could be struck at any moment by an earthquake with the force of 10 or 11 on the Richter scale. This would undoubtedly have cost many millions of lives.

A research team in Pasadena, using radio telescopes to calculate the exact distance between certain localities, made several disquieting discoveries. Research leader Peter MacDoran established that within 7 months the distance between two of the telescopes, one in Pasadena and one in Goldstone, had increased by 20 cm. and that, taking into account that the original distance was 180 km, and the usual slowness of such changes, was considered to be proof of unusual subterranean activity.

252

Suddenly however, and completely inexplicably to the experts, the accumulation of pressure under the San Andreas fault began to decrease. Within the space of a few weeks the situation had reversed itself to what it was in January 1979. The experts declared that there was no longer any danger of an imminent disaster, but could find no explanation for this sudden reversal.

It is understandable that they did not relate this to the eruption of the volcano Mt. St. Helens, which occurred, totally unexpectedly, at about the same time. Yet that was the outlet through which the accumulated pressure under the earth's crust was released due to the intervention of Maitreya and His group of Masters.

Contrary to the many pessimistic predictions it can safely be said that, because His work as the Agent of Divine Intervention will continue, California will not be struck by this major earthquake. On the contrary, all these events form an extra indication of the truth of this message of hope. The physical presence in the everyday world of the Christ is the guarantee that man will not destroy himself in a series of unprecedented disasters.

If we heed Maitreya's appeal for sharing, justice, brotherhood and love, we stand on the threshold of an era of unparalleled peace and progress.

Editor's note: Appendix to 2nd edition written, November, 1980, by Peter Liefhebber and Benjamin Creme.

For additional information,
tapes and booklets
write to:

TARA CENTER
P.O. Box 6001
North Hollywood, CA 91603
U.S.A.

TETRAHEDRON (see page 17)

SUGGESTED FURTHER READING

Alice A. Bailey, *Initiation, Human and Solar* (London: Lucis Press, 1922)

Alice A. Bailey, *The Externalisation of the Hierarchy* (London: Lucis Press, 1957)

Alice A. Bailey, *The Reappearance of the Christ* (London: Lucis Press, 1948)

H. P. Blavatsky, *The Secret Doctrine* (London: Theosophical Publishing House, 1888)

H. P. Blavatsky, *Isis Unveiled* (London: Theosophical Publishing House, 1877)

A. P. Sinnett, *The Mahatma Letters* (London: Theosophical Publishing House, 1923)

Baird T. Spalding, *Life and Teachings of the Masters of the Far East* (De Vorss & Co., Calif. U.S.A. 1924–55)

Paramhansa Yogananda, *Autobiography of a Yogi* (London: Rider, 1950)

M. Macdonald-Baine, *Beyond the Himalayas* (London: Fowler & Co.)

Swami Omananda, *Towards the Mysteries* (London: Neville Spearman, 1968)

Agni Yoga Teachings (various works) (New York: Agni Yoga Society, 1924–37)

Vera Stanley Alder, *The Initiation of the World* (London: Rider, 1939)

Vera Stanley Alder, *Humanity Comes of Age* (London: Rider, 1950)